Praise for *The Characters of Easter*

Dan Darling is such a delight to read! With eloquence and clarity, he gives us a tour of the many characters who witnessed the most important event in human history—Jesus' resurrection. Readers will be blessed to pick up this book!

JONATHAN PENNINGTON
Professor of New Testament at Southern Seminary; Spiritual Formation Pastor, Sojourn East

How often do we know the style and traditions of Easter, pastel colors, spring dresses, and seersucker suits, more than we know the actual characters involved in the story of our Lord's resurrection? The ultimate importance of Easter is that the tomb is empty, but there is so much more to the story that Dan Darling unlocks to help us see the significance of all those involved in the story leading up to the Super Bowl of Christianity, the resurrection of Jesus Christ. I'm looking forward to using *The Characters of Easter* as a primary reference for preaching a sermon series leading up to Easter, and I'm thankful he wrote this book.

DEAN INSERRA
Author of *The Unsaved Christian*; founding pastor of City Church Tallahasee

How fitting that a book about the resurrection makes the characters come alive! In *The Characters of Easter*, Dan Darling manages to make the most important theological event in history equally accessible to the person who's learning the story for the first time and the seasoned theologian who has studied it carefully for years. Filled with thoughtful and practical insights, this book will fuel the reader's passion for the passion story.

HERSHAEL W. YORK
Dean of the School of Theology and Professor of Preaching at The Southern Baptist Theological Seminary; Senior Pastor of Buck Run Baptist Church

I don't know how it happened. But somewhere along the way, I became numb to the wonder of Easter. I still believed that Jesus rose from the grave, but the miracle no longer moved and amazed me the way it once did. *The Characters of Easter* was the perfect antidote for my spiritual stupor. Darling's vivid portraits of the people present at the first Easter brought the momentous event to life for me. I learned fascinating details about the ancient world and received fresh insights about Jesus' friend and enemies. In the end, *The Characters of Easter* renewed my gratitude for Christ's sacrifice and resurrection and left me worshiping in the light of the empty tomb. I know it will do the same for you.

DREW DYCK
Editor; author of *Your Future Self Will Thank You: Secrets to Self-Control from the Bible and Brain Science*

THE CHARACTERS *of* EASTER

The Villains, Heroes, Cowards, and Crooks
Who Witnessed History's Biggest Miracle

DANIEL DARLING

MOODY PUBLISHERS
CHICAGO

Edited by Elizabeth Cody Newenhuyse
Interior design: Puckett Smartt
Cover design: Thinkpen Design
Cover illustration of Roman emperor copyright © 2019 by lynea / Shutterstock (92305465).
Cover illustration of spartan copyright © 2019 by Digital Storm / Shutterstock (363272741).
Cover illustration of sack copyright © 2019 by Uncle Leo / Shutterstock (469016627).
Cover illustration of bearded men copyright © 2019 by ArtMari / Shutterstock (646858039).
Cover illustration of women copyright © 2019 by ArtMari / Shutterstock (1086734156).
Cover illustration of nomad copyright © 2019 by ArtMari / Shutterstock (1752240242).
All rights reserved for all of the images above..

Library of Congress Cataloging-in-Publication Data

Names: Darling, Daniel, 1978- author.
Title: The characters of Easter : the villains, heroes, cowards, and crooks who witnessed history's biggest miracle / Daniel Darling.
Description: Chicago : Moody Publishers, [2021] | Includes bibliographical references. | Summary: "In The Characters of Easter, you'll become acquainted with the unlikely collection of ordinary people who witnessed the miracle of Christ's death and resurrection. Enter their stories and ultimately draw closer to Christ Himself as you encounter His Passion through their experiences"-- Provided by publisher.
Identifiers: LCCN 2020036953 (print) | LCCN 2020036954 (ebook) | ISBN 9780802423641 (paperback) | ISBN 9780802499721 (ebook)
Subjects: LCSH: Jesus Christ--Friends and associates. | Jesus Christ--Crucifixion. | Jesus Christ--Resurrection. | Jesus Christ--Ascension. | Jesus Christ--Appearances.
Classification: LCC BT590.F7 D37 2021 (print) | LCC BT590.F7 (ebook) | DDC 232.96--dc23
LC record available at https://lccn.loc.gov/2020036953
LC ebook record available at https://lccn.loc.gov/2020036954

Originally delivered by fleets of horse-drawn wagons, the affordable paperbacks from D. L. Moody's publishing house resourced the church and served everyday people. Now, after more than 125 years of publishing and ministry, Moody Publishers' mission remains the same—even if our delivery systems have changed a bit. For more information on other books (and resources) created from a biblical perspective, go to www.moodypublishers.com or write to:

Moody Publishers
820 N. LaSalle Boulevard
Chicago, IL 60610

1 3 5 7 9 10 8 6 4 2

Printed in the United States of America

This book is dedicated to my wonderful wife, Angela, who kept the home fires burning while I spent day and night working on this manuscript on a short deadline and during a global pandemic.

CONTENTS

Introduction: Why We Need Easter   9

1. The Failure: Peter   17

2. The Beloved: John   41

3. The Betrayer: Judas   65

4. The Rogue: Barabbas   85

5. The Powerless: Pilate   101

6. The Doubter: Thomas   121

7. The Religious: The Pharisees, Scribes, and Sadducees   137

8. The Witnesses: The Women at the Tomb   153

9. The Secret Disciples: Nicodemus and Joseph of Arimathea   169

10. The Executioners: Who Were the Romans?   183

Epilogue   197

Acknowledgments   199

Notes   201

Why We Need Easter

If Christ is risen, nothing else matters. And if Christ is not risen—
nothing else matters.[1]

JAROSLAV PELIKAN

And if Christ has not been raised, your faith is worthless; you are
still in your sins . . . If we have put our hope in Christ for this life
only, we should be pitied more than anyone.

1 CORINTHIANS 15:17, 19

I'm writing this during the strangest, hardest Easter I've ever experienced. Unlike the previous forty-one Easters in my life, our family won't be dressing up in our best church clothes. We won't be gathering with our friends and family at church. Instead, we are sitting on our couches in our living room watching a live stream.

In 2020 this is the reality for millions of Christians around the world as a deadly contagion spreading death and disease around the globe has kept us home, safe, so we don't spread it to the most vulnerable. It's necessary and it's right, but it's excruciating.

I'm writing with anticipation that when this book is published in early 2021, we have gotten a handle on the virus with antiviral medications and vaccines and are free, once again, to gather with brothers and sisters and worship our risen Savior. Likely, a year later, you have vivid memories of our most unusual 2020. Most of us will look back at a holiday spent at home. But for many, you might be recalling harrowing days and nights on the front lines, helping patients affected with COVID-19 get a few more desperate breaths. Or you might have been one of the important frontline workers who worked hard so we could pick up our prescriptions and have our food delivered to us and receive uninterrupted electricity and internet service. And it could be that Easter 2020 was the beginning of a bleak economic season, one that had you closing up your business or filing for unemployment benefits.

But as I write, it strikes me that while I'm despairing about missing out on the joy of Easter worship this year, the meaning of Easter has never been more relevant than it is this "plague year."

You need to know up front that I believe deep in my bones that the message we celebrate every spring is not a mere feel-good religious balm or a set of moral principles. No, it's more than that. We lament and rejoice, sing and sit silent, worship and wait because of a singular fact that changed the world: An itinerant rabbi from Nazareth named Jesus is the Son of God, human and divine, who took on the sins of a corrupted world and a broken humanity on a cruel Roman cross and then walked out of a borrowed tomb three days later, defeating the sin, death, and decay from which our pain arises.

Easter centers us in our pain, a fresh reminder that the ugliness of a fallen world—where sin's tentacles reach into every part of life, bringing death and despair to every corner of the world—has an expiration date.

In good times we too often sanitize Calvary's cross, treating it like a mere decorative icon topping steeples and hung in sanctuaries. Or, perhaps, worn around our necks. But the real cross was a sadistic instrument of torture and execution, a vile and inhumane way for an oppressive state to administer punishment and preserve order around the Empire.

Let's not forget what we are looking at when we look at the Passion. Jesus was beaten so badly as to be unrecognizable, stripped naked, forced to carry that same cross up a hill as throngs wept and jeered and stared, and then nailed to that same ugly piece of wood outside Jerusalem. And yet . . . here, in literally the worst thing that ever happened in human history, is life. In the death of this innocent man is the death of death. This is the answer from a God who hates death. In 1 Corinthians 15, we are told death is the "last enemy," an evil that has wormed its way through creation and infected human hearts since Eden. Sometimes Christians paper over death as if it's just a window into eternity, but we see that Jesus wept and was angry when He peered over and looked in on the corpse of His friend Lazarus.

On Good Friday, when we read Jesus' gasping words, "It is finished," know that in His agony is hope, death has lost its sting, and that one day, not long from now, we will see physical bodies rise to something new and beautiful.

✦ **Alone, So You Wouldn't Be** ✦

The most tragic reality of last Easter and too many other Easters is that so many people spend holidays like this alone, with no human connection; 2020 was agonizing because it brought funerals where loved ones couldn't gather to mourn loss, empty bedsides where those gasping for air were denied comforting touch, and long months when the elderly were isolated from meaningful community.

Humans are intensely social creatures, not made for isolation. On Good Friday, we can see in the agony of Jesus in His dying moments a true loneliness we are spared from experiencing. Jesus—the blame of humankind's worst evil thrust upon His sagging shoulders—felt the cold shoulder of the Father, who turned His face away. Jesus was alone so you would never be alone and could enjoy communion with the One who created you.

He felt the sting of isolation so you could be baptized into a body of believers in Heaven and earth. Jesus took upon Himself your sins so you could enjoy intimacy with your Father. He is the One who broke through the sting of death, who defeated sin, and who ushers you into communion with God.

To the grief-stricken sisters of Lazarus, Jesus gave this promise: "I am the resurrection and the life. The one who believes in me will live, even though they die" (John 11:25 NIV).

Jesus isn't only predicting that He would rise again. Jesus is saying more than that: He *is* the resurrection and the life. And this is why everything we say and believe hinges on this one reality. It separates Christianity from just another fantasy or religious exercise. Tish Warren writes poignantly, "It's painfully clear that the Resurrection is either the whole hope of the world—the very center of reality—or Christianity is not worth our time."[2]

This Easter we are declaring that it is worth our time because the Easter story is declaring that Jesus put death to death. It means that the curse that takes mothers and fathers, husbands and wives, children and grandchildren, coworkers and neighbors isn't eternal.

Consider the words of Paul, the educated, elite religious leader who once thought this new Jesus movement was a dangerous fad and a fool's errand. After his own encounter with the risen Jesus, he writes passionately in the most eloquent apologetic for Easter, in 1 Corinthians 15, why Jesus' resurrection changes everything:

> *But as it is, Christ has been raised from the dead, the firstfruits of those who have fallen asleep. For since death came through a man, the resurrection of the dead also comes through a man. For just as in Adam all die, so also in Christ all will be made alive. (vv. 20–22)*

Easter means those who are in Christ will be made alive, spiritually and physically. It means there is a new world dawning that is better than the old one. It means there is something afoot in the world. In the words of N. T. Wright, "Jesus's resurrection is the beginning of God's new project not to snatch people away from earth to heaven but to colonize earth with the life of heaven."[3]

Perhaps it's hard to make sense of it all, in the midst of whatever hardship or difficulty you are facing at the moment. The world, perhaps your world even, seems as upside down and unstable as it has ever been. But if the resurrection really happened, then it means this reality isn't forever.

Easter is the sign that a new world is coming, that one day God will take rotted dust particles, ravaged by disease and decay, and will reconstitute them into real, physical bodies fit for eternity. This cycle of pain and sadness, viruses and death has an expiration date.

✦　Join The Characters　✦

So, in this season let us peer in once again on a story we know so well. At the center of Easter, at the center of gravity of world history and of the cosmos, stands Jesus. But let's learn more about Christ by learning about the ragtag cast of characters who were swept up into His story. By looking at unlikely disciples, unprepared civil authorities, and unscrupulous religious leaders, we learn more about the setting in which Jesus lived and died, and we will gain a great love for God's long and sure plan of salvation and rescue.

We know and believe, as Peter declared on the day of Pentecost, that Easter was not an accident or series of unfortunate events, but that every single frame in the Easter drama is part of God's eternal plan from creation, when He prophesied that the seed of the woman and the seed of the serpent would violently clash until one day the serpent's head would be crushed (Gen. 3:15). Peter on the day of Pentecost articulates Easter's paradox:

> *"Though he was delivered up according to God's determined plan and foreknowledge, you used lawless people to nail him to a cross and kill him. God raised him up, ending the pains of death, because it was not possible for him to be held by death." (Acts 2:23–24)*

The plan of God and the actions and choices of humans—this is what we will explore this Easter. I want us to get inside these lives in this grand, cosmic drama. A young and unlikely band of disciples, corrupt rulers, brave women, and criminals who found freedom. Who are they?

Let's remember, if we can, that in the first century few understood the significance of what was happening. Israel was a forgotten backwater, an outpost where no aspiring Roman up-and-comer wanted to be exiled. And among the Jewish people there was widespread cynicism and despair. Tish Warren again reminds us of the setting:

> That morning in history when Jesus rose, there was no expectation of a resurrection. There was no fanfare. No churches gathering with songs of triumph, no bells ringing, nothing. A few women went out to tend to Jesus' dead body. His "nobody" disciples were laying low, lost in grief and feeling afraid. The rest of Jerusalem and the wider world had moved on. The sun rose. People went about their business gathering grain and water from wells. They started breakfast.[4]

All of the cosmos was changed, and it was almost entirely overlooked.

Easter was a surprise to those who first experienced it. For us, it's a familiar, even comforting ritual of sacred truth. But let's try our best to journey back to that setting and be willing to be surprised as well, to let the story of the resurrection wash over us anew.

CHAPTER ONE

The Failure

Peter

After Peter came to recognize his own inadequacy, his utter inability to fulfill his destiny apart from obedience to his only true responsibility, he became a rock-solid leader. As his story unfolds in the book of Acts, we can clearly see that when Peter kept his eyes on Jesus and followed Him, others followed too. And they followed by the thousands. Needed today: more Peters.[1]

CHARLES R. SWINDOLL

Simon Peter answered, "Lord, to whom will we go? You have the words of eternal life. We have come to believe and know that you are the Holy One of God."

JOHN 6:68–69

When Jesus met Simon, he wasn't the Peter we know, the saint after whom children and churches and cities are named. He was Simon and he wasn't exactly looking for Jesus. Instead, he was busy plying his trade as a commercial fisherman on the shores of Lake Gennesaret. Simon and his brother Andrew were part of a fishing collective with another set of brothers, James and John. The Galilee shores were all the brothers knew, having grown up in Bethsaida, on the northwest shore.

By all accounts, Simon was thriving in Capernaum, making a living bringing fish to the market to be sold locally or shipped to Damascus via the Roman highway and exported to ports across the Roman Empire along the Mediterranean. He owned a home and was married (Luke 4:38–39). It doesn't seem like Simon was either rich or poor but managing a decent life. Like most of us: an ordinary person in an ordinary place in what, he assumed, was an ordinary time.

Jesus spent much of His ministry in Galilee. These were His people: blunt, salt-of-the-earth, and hardworking. Galileans didn't much care for the elite sophisticates in Jerusalem, and the elites returned the scorn. A son of Nazareth in the southwest part of the Galilee region, Jesus made Capernaum His base of operation. Just as God chose a humble place—Bethlehem—for the entrance of Jesus into the world, so the Master Craftsman chose to build His new movement from the raw and rugged people of Galilee. This is not where you would typically recruit if you were building a movement that would shake the world, but Christ often draws His disciples from out-of-the-way places.

We don't really know when Jesus arrived in town. Did He ever pass Simon in the marketplace or sit next to him in the synagogue? In everyday interactions, they would not have noticed anything unusual about this carpenter in town. Jesus didn't have a halo above His head and an arrow pointing to His face, letting people know He was God's Son. It seems that Jesus' pursuit of Peter came patiently, in a series of fits and starts, like He seems to come to all of us, a conversation here, a conversation there. But make no mistake that the "Hound of Heaven," named by C. S. Lewis and the poet Francis Thompson, persistently pursued this prickly Galilean.

✦ **When Jesus Met Peter** ✦

The first encounter seems to have been brokered by Simon's brother Andrew. He was intrigued with another itinerant teacher, the rogue prophet named John. Some called him "the baptizer" for his controversial practice of calling Jewish people to a new level of repentance and cleansing, beyond the cold rituals. John was unlike the staid rabbis in the synagogue. A wild-eyed nomad who declared the kingdom of heaven had come near, John insisted the people of God must prepare themselves. While many shrugged off John's message, Andrew listened. And the words cut straight to his heart. John didn't speak of himself, but of another whom God was sending, with a winnowing fork, dividing true believers from pretenders. A more radical, powerful baptism was coming, one of spirit and fire. Andrew wasn't sure he knew exactly what John meant, but he had a strange attraction to the message.

How did Simon feel about Andrew's fascination with this new movement? We don't know what those conversations on the water were like, but it does seem that Simon hung back a bit. Did he think Andrew was getting involved in some dangerous new movement? Did he write John the Baptist off as another fad, soon to fade from a first-century scene that featured so many religious imposters and would-be messiahs? Did he roll his eyes at Andrew's new ideas, the way we roll our eyes when a crazy uncle posts a conspiracy theory on the internet?

Galileans were ready for messages about God's coming kingdom, especially at a time when Israel keenly felt the burden of being a subject people. But hope for a better future was shadowed by a palpable sense of despair, a cynicism hardened by crushing Roman rule and failed revolutions. In their lifetime, Galileans had been massacred in an ugly confrontation with the governor of Judea, Pontius Pilate.

And yet Andrew was still listening that one day, during a trip to Jerusalem with John, when the prophet pointed at a fellow Galilean, the son of Joseph, and declared of Jesus, "Look, the Lamb of God, who takes away the sin of the world!" Andrew went to the place where Jesus was staying and was captivated by this rabbi's teaching. So he returned to Capernaum and ran toward his brother Simon and urged him to check out this Jesus.

You can almost picture the scene in your mind, can't you? "We have found the Messiah," John 1:41 records Andrew saying, but I see him shouting, breathless and grabbing Simon by his fishing vest. *This is the one! I know it sounds crazy. But trust me, you've got to come hear Him and see Him. I've never seen anything like this.*

Messiah, *anointed one*, meant a lot of things; and while the two brothers were catechized in the Torah, they were not scholars who pored over texts. And yet, unlike those who did, they knew enough to follow. They didn't and wouldn't understand then that the Christ would not just swoop in and conquer Israel's enemies. They couldn't see an unjust trial, a bloody cross, and the sending of the Spirit. But they knew just enough to follow.

✦ Found! ✦

I think a lot about those simple words Andrew said that day. *We have found Him.* Are these not the words that beckon us every year to

Easter? Are these not the words that one friend says to another, up-ending future generations? I think of my own father, who heard these words from my aunt who watched when an evangelist named Billy Graham spoke them to her on TV. My father walked that aisle in 1971 in Chicago and changed the trajectory of his troubled family. I'm here today, writing books for Easter, because my father heard those words and said them to a young Jewish girl who would become his wife, a mother who would tell her son one day: *We have found Him.*

Of course when Andrew and Simon found Jesus, they didn't know all that this would mean. And neither do we when we with knocking knees walk the aisle, or with trembling lips bow our heads, or feel, like John Wesley, strangely warmed. Some find Jesus on the side of the road, some after a drunken haze in a dorm room, some after late-night conversations with friends. Some find Jesus in rehab, others in church, and still others, like renowned scientist Francis Collins, find Jesus at the end of a test tube.

But the important thing is: you found Him. And yet as much as it seems we found Jesus, it was really Jesus who was doing the looking.

John preached. Andrew listened. John pointed to Jesus. Andrew *found.* This is how the gospel reaches you and it reaches me. God sends someone to us: a voice on the radio, a discarded tract, a persistent friend. It seems so random, and yet when we look back we see how Providence unfolds mysteriously and makes its way to us.

Simon didn't know it, but his life story was being written before he was born. It began miles away in tiny Bethlehem thirty years earlier, when an impoverished carpenter and his wife pounded on the doors of an inn, begging for a place to give birth to their baby. Simon's story began when an aging priest named Zechariah and his wife, Elizabeth, miraculously conceived and bore a child born to be a prophet. Jesus, John the Baptist, and Simon would converge, not by accident or fate, but by the silent fingers of God. The fullness of time was coming to bear down on an unsuspecting young fisherman.

And it was on the day Simon reluctantly followed that the entrepreneur fisherman became, in Jesus' words, Peter—meaning "rock" (Matt. 16:18). Yes, the one who had to be dragged to Jesus would become a pillar of God's new creation movement in the world, would be written into salvation history as one of the twelve Apostles, and would write two letters that would become Holy Writ. Jesus' closest companions, tasked with the founding of the church, would not be drafted from the finest rabbinical schools or from among the educated scribes or the bluebloods in Herod's court, but would be plucked, like so many of Israel's leaders, from the ranks of the common. The kingdom of God seems to travel away from the places of power and toward the unheralded, the unseen, the unqualified. The carpenter King, born in poverty on the backside of nobility, seeks His followers among those whom the world does not see.

✦ Pursuing Peter ✦

That dramatic first encounter with Andrew in Jerusalem was only the first of many appeals by Jesus to Peter. One day Jesus appeared on the shores of Galilee while the two brothers worked the deep waters for another day's catch (Matt. 4; Mark 1). "Follow me," the Master called, "and I'll make you fishers of men" (Matt. 4:19 ESV). What did "follow me" mean? He didn't know, but Peter followed anyway as Jesus taught and healed and preached in Peter's own synagogue in Capernaum (Luke 4:31).

Jesus became more familiar with Peter, staying in his home (Luke 4:38) and healing his mother-in-law of a fever, no small malady in a time before pain relievers, antibiotics, and vaccines. Peter's home became a gathering place of sorts as word spread throughout Capernaum, and others made their way to his home, the desperate seeking healing and hope from this new rabbi.

Imagine what this must have been like for Peter to experience. What questions rattled around his head? For us, reading the text today, two thousand years removed, these biblical scenes of healing don't pack the wallop they must have for those who witnessed such events. But for Peter, this was completely new. In Peter's time the blind never saw. The lame never walked. The demons never left.

While Jesus is teaching and healing, He's also pursuing Peter. One day, after Peter returns from an unsuccessful overnight fishing trip, Jesus appears again on the beach and crowds began to form, eager to listen to His teaching. So Jesus asked the brothers to lend their boat to use as a place to sit and teach the gathering crowds. The brothers' grimy and smelly boat—now a stage for the Son of God. And when the crowd dispersed, Jesus urged the men to give the nets another chance.

The Scripture suggests this tip rankled Peter, and we know why. When an amateur weighs in on our area of expertise, it raises our hackles. These guys knew the lake better than almost anyone. They were good at fishing, having spent their whole lives mastering the currents, discerning where schools of fish gathered and when exactly to cast their nets and when to draw them in. This was their business, their livelihood, their way of life. Jesus—He's good for miracles and messages, but why was He messing with their business? Imagine

LeBron James being told how to make a game-winning shot or Tiger Woods how to sink an eighteen-foot putt at the Masters or Dr. Fauci being told by one of your crazy uncles on Facebook how to diagnose infectious diseases. Peter didn't say it, but you know the internal dialogue went something like this: *Jesus, You know nothing about this business. I've been doing this my whole life. It's just not a good day out here. We'll come back and get it tomorrow.*

And yet Peter would learn, as do all who follow Jesus, that the Master is not just interested in our Sunday morning piety, but He demands lordship over all of our lives, even and maybe especially those areas we have mastered. He's a Monday-through-Friday kind of Lord.

This is what Jesus was doing with Peter that day. And to Peter's credit, he acquiesced, "If you say so," the CSB translation renders Luke's Greek. You can feel the sigh here, a grudging, shoulders-slumped kind of obedience. But he grabbed those nets, those nets he had already cleaned and stowed away, and slung them over the side of the boat.

What followed was, well, a miracle. You can quibble about the shape of the miracle: Was this the Lord of Creation, fashioning hundreds of prize tilapia, carp, and sardines in an instant? Or the Lord of Creation directing hundreds of prize tilapia, carp, and sardines to obey the voice of their Creator and swim toward nets?

What we do know is that in this seemingly ordinary moment, on a bad day at the office, Jesus opens up the heavens, just a crack, to show a group of shaken fishermen a glimpse of His divine power. As we've seen, Peter had witnessed miracles from Jesus before. But this was different. Here was Jesus in Peter's boat, in the one arena where Peter was master, in the area of his life that Peter had tucked away as his own. This was not someone else's miracle he was witnessing.

This was *Peter's* miracle. An empty net and an empty lake suddenly, inexplicably full of fish. Peter knew the sea, but Jesus *made* the sea.

There was a message in the miracle. Jesus is reassuring Peter that he could leave behind his profitable business and follow. That boatful of fish was a check in the mail at just the right time, a yield that would perhaps give him enough money to care for his family while he was on the road with Jesus. He had heard Jesus say to seek first the kingdom of God and all these things—important things like money and family and future—would be taken care of (Matt. 6:33). Peter could afford to deny himself, to leave father and mother, to abandon investments where moth and rust corrupt and where thieves break through and steal. A disciple of Christ can entrust those things that keep us up at night to the God who never sleeps. Not a promise of prosperity, of course, but a promise of provision.

But Jesus was delivering an even clearer message. This was a vision of Peter's future life. He was the empty net God would one day fill with spiritual power to preach to thousands of people at Pentecost, lead the early church, and write two books of inspired biblical canon.

Peter's response in this moment is really the only appropriate response when confronted with Jesus: he bowed and worshiped Jesus. "Go away from me, because I'm a sinful man, Lord!" (Luke 5:8). You'll notice that nobody in Scripture is ever casual after an encounter with the living God: Moses glowed, Isaiah was "undone," Ezekiel face-planted in fear, John fainted. Peter was overwhelmed—but he left his nets and followed.

✦   Where Else Would We Go?   ✦

Following Jesus took Peter across Galilee and Judea and to places he could have never imagined. Lepers healed. Lame walking. The blind receiving sight. He saw Jesus raise a servant girl from the dead. Peter was there, twice, when the Lord of Creation scooped up a little boy's lunch and stretched it to feed thousands of hungry, desperate people, with food left over. And there was the time Jesus, awoke from a nap and saved the disciples from shipwreck by speaking, yes speaking, to the water and turning a choppy sea smooth as glass in an instant.

There were also many moments that Peter just didn't understand, such as Jesus' insistence on going through Samaria, where no Galilean ever set foot. And not only did He pass through Samaria, He initiated a conversation with a sketchy woman who astonishingly became an evangelist. He heard Jesus describe the faith of a Roman centurion, the very symbol of oppression and power, as the greatest faith in all of Israel. And there was the time Jesus insisted on dining with the traitorous tax collectors.

It seemed the more Peter messed up, the more Jesus drew him into the inner circle.

And it seemed the more Peter messed up, the more he opened his mouth before his brain engaged, the more Jesus drew him into the inner circle. Peter was the only one who, when he saw Jesus walking on the water toward them, didn't stay in the boat to gaze on the miracle but impulsively leapt into the sea and began walking on the water himself (Matt. 14:29). Peter was the one who, when Jesus took him and James and John to the top of a mountain and revealed to them a glimpse of His divine glory, suggested they domesticate the

Transfiguration with a series of memorials, and was rebuked by the Father (Matt. 17:1–4; Mark 9:2–5; Luke 9:32–33).

Perhaps nothing encapsulates what this three-year journey was like for this fisherman-turned-follower than the words he spoke in response to a haunting question. After thousands of fair-weather followers peeled away from their movement in response to some hard teaching, Jesus offered a most human question: "You don't want to go away too, do you?" (John 6:67). Jesus, Son of God, knew His mission and journeyed toward the cross, but Jesus, Man of Sorrows, was hurt as people rejected Him. In this moment, Peter spoke up:

> *Simon Peter answered, "Lord, to whom will we go? You have the words of eternal life. We have come to believe and know that you are the Holy One of God." (John 6:68–69)*

To whom will we go? This is why we pause every spring and gaze at a bloody cross and an empty tomb; why we drag ourselves out of bed on cold Sunday mornings, week after week; why, weary and sorrowful and not sure about anything, we come to Jesus in jumbled prayer. We have nowhere else to go, no one else to turn to. Jesus has the words of eternal life.

What Peter had was a tiny seed of faith, implanted in him by the Spirit of God. We know this because we read his bold words of affirmation of Jesus as the Christ, the anointed one spoken of by the Old Testament prophets. Jesus, standing at Caesarea Philippi, on the ruins of ancient temples where sacrifices to the pagan gods had been offered, had pressed into His disciples and had asked them, "Who do you say I am?" (Matt. 16:15–16; Mark 8:29; Luke 9:20). Peter answered the question that, sooner or later, every human soul must answer. "You are the Christ, the Son of the living God" (ESV).

He didn't understand everything. Peter couldn't imagine the Messiah King as a crucified, arrested Lord. He didn't like Jesus' prediction of death and resurrection for Himself, hardly the career trajectory of a triumphant conqueror. In fact, not long after his declaration of faith, Peter was rebuked by Jesus for opposing the journey to the cross. Peter's vision of God's kingdom involved blood, yes, but surely it would be Roman blood spilled underfoot as the righteous King put down the Roman overlords. He could not see ahead the blood of the One he loved splattered across an ugly instrument of torture and death. But make no mistake: Peter's open declaration of Jesus as God's Son was not the safe choice. It defied the religious leaders. Soon the crowds would be howling for Jesus' death. And one day this simple declaration would make Peter an enemy of Rome.

With twenty-first-century hindsight, expressed in air-conditioned auditoriums and comfortable seating, we don't fully grasp what it would mean for a respectable Jewish businessman to sacrifice his reputation and openly declare that this teacher from Nazareth was God Himself, in the flesh. We can't feel the sting of social isolation Peter and others would endure in the years ahead, alienation from their own family and tribe and eventual martyrdom.

Jesus' response was that upon this rock—yes, Peter the impulsive, impatient, imperfect disciple—Christ would build His church. Peter and the other disciples would become Apostles, ushering in a new age of salvation history.

✦ I've Got This, Lord ✦

Which bring us, ultimately, to the life-defining moment of Peter's story. It's a story included in all four gospels so we know it was important to the gospel writers who wrote their eyewitness accounts under inspiration of the Holy Spirit following decades of oral tradition in the early church. You can't tell the Easter story without talking about Peter's stunning denial.

How could a devoted disciple suddenly turn on Jesus? To understand, I think we have to step into his sandals on that tragic early morning. The scenes of denial come toward the end of a long and emotionally draining week that began with great joy and promise.

Jesus and the disciples had arrived the Friday before in Bethany, a small community within walking distance of Jerusalem. The week ahead would feel more like a year. It would begin with an emotional high, with Jesus triumphantly entering the city on a donkey and being hailed by crowds of palm-branch-waving supporters as the King of the Jews. Jesus was fulfilling Zechariah's prophecy of an unorthodox future king who would ride into Jerusalem, not in a chariot, but on a humble beast of burden.

Then there was a joyous meal at Simon the leper's house where Mary opened an expensive bottle of perfume and washed Jesus' feet in a display of extravagance that Peter couldn't understand and enraged Judas. But Jesus embraced Mary's gesture as a sign that she understood, unlike the others, what was to unfold in the coming days.

How could a devoted disciple suddenly turn on Jesus?

As the days wore on, there was a growing sense of danger. Whispers of plots by religious leaders, secret schemes to capture Jesus and the disciples. Word came of a conspiracy to capture and kill Lazarus, whom Jesus had raised from the dead. It must have frustrated Peter and the other disciples that Jesus seemed to do nothing to tamp down danger or to fight back. At times, Jesus seemed to exacerbate the division, chasing out the merchants and the grifters from the temple and predicting that Herod's magnificent edifice, Israel's source of national pride, would be unceremoniously destroyed in the not-so-distant future.

One night, Jesus gathered them at the Mount of Olives and communicated His vision for the future of Israel, of the disciples' movement into the world. If Peter was looking for immediate revolution against their enemies, he surely came away disappointed. But Jesus talked of both His impending death and of a second coming, this time in judgment. If, all these centuries later, Christians still seem perplexed by the future, imagine how the disciples felt on that chilly night.

It all climaxed, however, when Jesus and the disciples enjoyed a Passover in a room that Peter and John had secured. This had all of the elements of a typical Passover meal, except Jesus continued to talk of His own coming arrest and death at the hands of His enemies. How could a king rule, Peter must have wondered, when He seemed so resigned to the fate of capture? But Jesus continued and mentioned His leaving them and the sending of the Spirit of God, a prospect that made them sad and a little angry.

Peter had left everything and had staked it all on the idea that Jesus was the promised Messiah. But how could the Messiah allow Himself to be captured and killed? Internally, Peter must have reassured himself that he wouldn't let this happen. He'd fight and give his life in order to protect his Master. But Jesus didn't seem to entertain Peter's delusions. He somberly predicted that all the disciples would desert Him, and one would even betray Him. It was like He could see into Peter's soul in a way Peter couldn't see himself:

> *"Simon, Simon, behold, Satan demanded to have you, that he might sift you like wheat, but I have prayed for you that your faith may not fail. And when you have turned again, strengthen your brothers." Peter said to him, "Lord, I am ready to go with you both to prison and to death." Jesus said, "I tell you, Peter, the rooster will not crow this day, until you deny three times that you know me."*
> *(Luke 22:31–34 ESV)*

After the Passover meal, Jesus asked Peter and James and John to join Him in the Garden of Gethsemane where Jesus went to pray. He asked them to wait for Him, to pray, at this late hour. They were weary. It was very late. Imagine how the roller-coaster of the last several days must have caught up with Peter. He was probably still trying to process the stunning exchange with Judas. The friend he had trusted, who had been side-by-side with them for three years, who had given up everything, would now sell Jesus out. He didn't want to believe it. So Peter drifted off to sleep, only to be awakened by the sight of an ashen, weary Jesus, tears and blood rolling down His face. His words pierced Peter's soul, *Could you not have prayed and watched?*

And then it happened so suddenly. Soldiers marching into the dark garden. Torches and swords. And . . . Judas, their friend, embracing Jesus in a final, sick display. The kiss of betrayal. Peter was so enraged, adrenaline flowing. His world spinning. His life coming unglued. This was so unfair. So unjust. So wrong. So he clumsily stole a sword and struck the high priest's servant. Jesus didn't accept Peter's defense of Him but instead healed the ear of His enemy.

The disciples, we are told in Matthew 25 and Mark 14, scattered. But Peter and John lingered, using John's connections to get into the courtyard where the secret and illegal trial of Jesus took place in Ananias's house. Should Peter have gone? What else could he do? He had to find a way to be near Jesus, to protect Him, to fight for Him, to demonstrate his loyalty.

The same impulsive faith that led him to leap out of the boat and walk on water, to blurt out an affirmation of Jesus' deity, was the same faith that kept Peter close when others fled. So Peter stands by a fire in the courtyard, probably a bit nervous. It's dark, so maybe they don't see him. Maybe he's trying to be inconspicuous, but it's impossible. A servant girl comes over and asks him, "You're one of those with Jesus of Nazareth, right?"

It could be that he's trying to shush her so others don't hear and his cover won't be blown, so he can stick around. But he's a fisherman, not a spy. He's Peter, the Galilean with the thick accent. So Peter dashes out of there and sort of lingers by the entrance.

Mark's gospel says that the first rooster crowed in this moment. A warning shot. But I'm not sure Peter even heard it. I think Peter waits out here a bit, watching to see if the coast is clear, then goes back to that fire. Remember it's cold out, probably forty degrees. And he wants to hear news. So he sneaks back into the courtyard again, trying not to be seen.

But he's no Navy SEAL or trained Roman operative. "This guy is with Jesus!" someone shouts. And again, he denies it. At this point, I still don't think Peter is trying to sell out Christ. I think he's still trying to stay close, so he can see what is happening. But this plan, this trust in his own instincts and bravery, is failing fast. To quote that twenty-first-century theologian, country singer Jason Isbell, Peter was telling himself, "[I] thought I was strong until I finally had to fight."[2]

One of the relatives of the servant whose ear was cut off by Peter says, "Didn't I see you with him in the garden?" At this point, Peter's cover is totally blown. He's exposed before his accusers and he panics. I mean, if your uncle's ear gets cut off, you recognize the guy who raised that sword so awkwardly against him, right? So Peter resorts to the language of the sea, spitting out curses, his old life tumbling back into the foreground. And it's in this moment of truth that the words Jesus spoke to him the night before echo back and pierce his soul. Another rooster crow.

The gospels all record their versions of this story, but Luke, the meticulous journalist, records a particularly haunting detail: somehow Peter was within eyeshot of Jesus. "Then the Lord turned and looked at Peter" (Luke 22:61). You can just read the hurt and ache in those words. The eye contact, the look of anguish on Jesus' face, the despair roiling now through Peter's heart. This once-proud, self-assured young man was fully and unreservedly broken. Luke later records that he "went out and wept bitterly" (Luke 22:62).

Have you ever had a moment when you wept bitterly? I have. A genuine confrontation with the cross of Christ will do this, exposing our pride and self-sufficiency, the sin that blackens our souls. Whether you approach Jesus with a record of accomplishment and a life of charity or you shuffle forward with halting steps and a life of shame, Calvary will break you, and yet it will lift you up.

And so we shouldn't see this as Peter's end, but the beginning of his life's work. Peter's failure here was not one of cowardice, but of pride. He had loyally stayed by Jesus' side far longer while others fled. Peter's failure was his inability to fully see himself. When Peter looked in the mirror every morning, he saw a strong, successful, brave warrior, but Jesus' piercing look that dark night revealed the real man: a weak and frail disciple.

The world would one day see a courageous Peter, resisting the government and boldly preaching the gospel to thousands. But it would be a different kind of courage, one that he would later define as truth wrapped in gentleness and kindness and buoyed not by own self-assurance, but the "living hope" of the resurrection of Jesus Christ (1 Peter 1:3). Peter would live the rest of his life with humility. That rooster crow he heard on the night of his denial? That was a common sound in the cacophony of daily life in Israel. So imagine every sunrise after that fateful day, he'd be reminded of his failure.

Like God's best servants, Peter would walk with a limp.

Like God's best servants, Peter would walk with a limp; he'd bear the scars of past failure. This is the same journey toward leadership we see throughout the Scriptures: Abraham had Ishmael, Jacob had a hollowed-out thigh bone, Moses a stutter, Paul a mysterious thorn in the flesh. We have to come to understand that our scars are not marks to be ashamed of, but gifts from God that remind us, daily, of our weaknesses.

This is hard for us to comprehend in a culture that continually tells us we are strong. We are catechized by inspirational mumbo-jumbo: *you are strong, you are brave, you've got this.* But real strength is found not in summoning some illusion of inner machismo. Instead, we, like Peter, need to be broken in order to be brave.

Peter's dramatic fall was the beginning of his rise. And we only know about the denial and the rooster crowing because Peter himself shared it. Nobody else from the inner circle was with him in the courtyard, by the fire, and outside the high priest's house. We can only read about it in the gospels because Peter must have shared it, over and over again, with audiences large and small until it became such a part of the eyewitness narratives that later became the gospels and inspired canon of Scripture. What's more, if Mark was the first gospel written, as many scholars believe, then this means Peter *intended* for God's people to see him at his worst moment.

We can only wonder how many thousands, perhaps millions, have converted to Christianity because this Apostle cut open his heart and shared his most vulnerable moment. Only heaven knows. So maybe it's time we stop looking at Peter as a foolish coward and instead see in this man an example of Christ's transformative gospel work. Peter's response to his sin, in contrast to that of the sad tale of Judas, is a study in true repentance. Like David's transparent confession in Psalm 51, we find no justifications, obfuscations, or anger. We just see a once-proud, self-confident man reduced to a mess of tears. This is why Jesus would name him "the rock," not because he was bursting with brava-do, but because of a tender, contrite heart.

Most importantly, Peter's denial shows us something about the Savior. Jesus, at a moment of extreme agony and personal shame, turned and looked with compassion at His friend who was at that moment sinning against Him. "While we were still sinners, Christ died for us" (Rom. 5:8). He didn't go to the cross for perfect, whole people. He died for the sick and the broken. He died for you and me.

Jesus, while predicting Peter's demise, also quietly said the words, "When you have turned back, strengthen your brothers." *When you have turned back.* Jesus saw through Peter's failures and toward his future as an Apostle. This is a word for Christians: The way to personal peace is through repentance and the way to restoration is to look at your Savior who has not turned away from you but has fresh reservoirs of grace.

And so it is, in this generation, God is calling flawed, broken, repentant people for His mission in the world.

✦ And . . . Peter ✦

We don't know where Peter went after his denial. He isn't present, like John and Jesus' mother Mary, at the foot of the cross while Jesus died. But we know he likely didn't go back home. Capernaum is about eighty miles from Jerusalem, a two-hour journey by car today and a four-day walk back then. Did he stay with friends Mary and Martha and Lazarus in Bethany?

What we do know is that the next couple of days must have been Peter's most difficult. Broken by his behavior the night of Jesus' arrest and unsure of what the future looks like, Peter was staring into an abyss of uncertainty. All that Jesus had promised during their last meal together, the passages we read in John 14–16, didn't make sense yet. The King he assumed would set up the kingdom of God and overthrow the Romans was decomposing in a borrowed tomb.

Unless, of course, He wasn't.

Peter's Sunday-morning misery was punctuated by a sudden visit from a breathless group of women led by Mary Magdalene and Mary, Jesus' mother. They could barely get the words out. What they said seemed crazy. No, actually it was crazy. The body of Jesus, gone? This was impossible. The tomb was guarded with tight Roman security. A heavy stone sealed the entrance. Oh, and there is this little detail that dead bodies don't just rise again. But the women were serious.

And they carried a word especially for Peter. Mark records a scene at the tomb where a man dressed in a white robe urges Mary, "Tell the disciples and Peter" (Mark 16:7).

And Peter. These two words had Peter rubbing the sleep out of his eyes and sprinting toward the cave where Joseph of Arimathea, a wealthy benefactor, paid to bury Jesus. When Peter arrived, he saw what the women had just seen: an empty hole, a rolled-away stone, and, most telling, Jesus' folded grave clothes.

Peter was probably never so happy to see a pile of used clothes. The neat folds, placed with intentionality, were clear evidence that Jesus had indeed slipped the bonds of death and was raised by the Father to life. This was a physical testimony to a physical resurrection.

We don't know where and when Jesus met up with Peter for the first time after the resurrection, but we can imagine the scene. Scripture records several other meetings with Jesus where Peter was likely present, twice in the Upper Room, another in Galilee as Jesus delivered the Great Commission mandate. Paul records later in 1 Corinthians 15:7 that Jesus made a personal appearance to Peter after the resurrection. Jesus, just as persistent in Peter's restoration as He was in his initial calling.

Peter's story climaxes in a scene John paints: an event on the beach that matches, almost perfectly, the description Luke gives us at the beginning of Peter's journey with Jesus. It's no mistake, no coincidence that the Master bookends His three years with Peter with the same miracle: a fruitless day of fishing, a reluctant toss of the nets to humor Jesus, and a boatload of fish.

John writes this scene with great detail. Here is Jesus physically feeding His disciples, a testament to a real resurrection of His body. Jesus is not a mystical disembodied angel, but a resurrected human.

There's fish to eat: humans eat, angels don't. This matters to us because it means if Jesus rose again, those who are in Him will also rise again, bodily.

And let's think about what memory a charcoal fire, the same kind of fire that was burning in that cold courtyard, would spark in Peter? The last time he warmed his hands, his heart turned cold toward Jesus. And yet this image is undoubtedly an image of hope. Peter may have abandoned Jesus in Jesus' hour of need, but Jesus would not abandon Peter in his hour of need. This is why Jesus asking Peter three times about the depth of his love is not a test of faithfulness as some imagine it, but God's way of calling this future Apostle to a life of service. The new way of leadership in the kingdom of God is not about position or title, but about humbly serving—feeding—the people of God. To love God is to love those God loves, and to declare what Peter knew: Christ defeated sin, death and the grave, and is saving sinners.

To love God is to love those God loves.

Christ is still seeking out fishers of men, the kind of leaders who walk with a limp. Here we see God's unmatched, one-way love. We fail Him, but He doesn't fail us. We forget Him, but He doesn't forget us. We pursue other loves, but He is faithful.

◆ An Empty Soul Is Filled ◆

Peter's life is one, really, of emptiness and filling: empty nets, empty self, empty tomb. An empty net is a sign of professional failure and for a successful Galilean merchant, there was no greater sign of loss than an empty net. An empty net meant nothing to sell and trade. It meant an empty wallet, empty stomachs, and an empty house. Jesus entered

Peter's life, at the very beginning of this call to ministry and at the very end, filling Peter's empty nets.

But this was only the smallest way Christ would fill the empty places in Peter's life. Peter's soul, that day on the beach, was also bereft. He had failed Jesus in the worst possible way in the worst moments. The news of the resurrection was both bitter and sweet. Sweet in that the one he loved was not held down by Roman nails and the devil's schemes. Bitter in that Peter would have to face the friend he betrayed. Yet it was another empty place—a borrowed tomb outside the city walls—that healed the shame in this disciple's soul. For Jesus, in walking out of that grave, walked into victory over sin, the sin that corrupts hearts and makes proud men cowards. Stripped of his self-assurance, bereft of confidence, shorn of pride, Peter could now be filled with a different kind of power, the one that saw him stand up to religious bullies, preach the gospel to thousands, and one day hang upside down for the same Lord he had earlier betrayed.

What gave Peter this courage? That look from Jesus in Jesus' moment of agony. The same kind of salvation that gives us courage. Years later, as an aging Apostle, he'd write: "He himself bore our sins in his body on the tree; so that, having died to sins, we might live for righteousness. By his wounds you have been healed" (1 Peter 2:24).

Peter could live for righteousness and we can live for righteousness, not because we summon up our own goodness or bravery, but because there was One who bore our own sins in His body on the tree. It is not until our nets our empty, until all of the self-saving, self-justifying, self-satisfying religion is gone and we are absolutely as low as we can go, that Jesus arrives and fills us with supernatural grace to let His life be lived through us.

STUDY QUESTIONS:

◆ Reread the narrative of Peter's first call and second call in Luke 5 and John 21. What does Jesus' pursuit of Peter tell us about the way God calls disciples?

◆ Think through the denial of Peter. Why do you suppose Peter insisted that he, unlike the other disciples, would be loyal and brave when Jesus needed him? What does that tell us about our own tendency to think we are stronger than we really are?

◆ In John 6:68, Peter says that he would follow Jesus because he had nowhere else to go. What does this tell us about the nature of faith?

SUGGESTED HYMNS AND SONGS:

And Can It Be That I Should Gain—Charles Wesley
How Can It Be—Lauren Daigle

The Beloved

John

*It is the unique, tender, genuine, chief Gospel . . . Should a tyrant
succeed in destroying the Holy Scriptures and only a single copy of
the Epistle to the Romans and the Gospel according to John escape
him, Christianity would be saved.*[1]

MARTIN LUTHER ON THE GOSPEL OF JOHN

*Dear friends, let us love one another, because love is from God,
and everyone who loves has been born of God and knows God.*

1 JOHN 4:7

It was an otherwise ordinary, cool spring night in Nashville when
we went to bed on March 1. On my mind as my head hit the pil-
low was the home stretch of our four kids' school season, a potential
job change, and a potential new Easter book (!) I was about to start
writing.

I am usually a very heavy sleeper, but I awoke around midnight
to hear an alarm on my wife's iPhone. I assumed that perhaps she had
accidentally set her morning alarm too early or that perhaps it was actually 5 a.m. It wasn't 5 a.m., and this wasn't the typical alarm. Angela

reached over and managed to fumble her way to turning off the noise. But then we heard sirens outside. So I sat up. Apparently, some kind of storm was making its way toward our community.

At first we kind of brushed off the alarms. Tennessee gets a lot of thunder and rain in the winter and spring, so much of the time we kind of ignore the warnings. But they kept going, so I finally got out of bed and grabbed my phone and checked a weather account on Twitter, @nashseverewx. The models had a tornado bearing down, not just on Nashville, but toward our exact community, perhaps even our subdivision. So we woke the kids and huddled in our downstairs bathroom. I'm glad we did.

Wind and rain lashed the house and before long, the power went out. Thunder rumbled overhead and then it got pretty quiet, which always makes me nervous. Then there was a sound that sounded like our clothes dryer in the next room over was kicking on, only this time with a cinder block inside. We realized then that this was the tornado passing right over our home.

We were spared, unlike many in our community. Friends had homes destroyed, their schools flattened and churches severely damaged. One sweet, elderly couple died in their home. It was a surreal experience to ride around the next day and see the widespread path of destruction. It's one thing to read about a tornado happening somewhere else. It is quite another to experience one in your own town.

Tornadoes, or any other kind of severe storm, are powerful and arouse great fear. We try to avoid them as much as we can and typically have to clean up after their destruction. So imagine a person whose personality is described in this way. You'd think they'd be the least likely person to be chosen as a spiritual leader, much less a pillar of the early church. And yet one of the most important characters in the Easter story, John, was given by Jesus the unflattering nickname of "Son of Thunder" (Mark 3:17).

◆ Dropping the Nets ◆

We find John in the same place we found Peter, plying his trade as a Galilean fisherman. He and his elder brother, James, ran a successful fishing enterprise in Capernaum owned by their father, Zebedee. John was the other disciple who accompanied Andrew in following John the Baptist, the wilderness prophet who barnstormed Israel with his unconventional lifestyle and an even more unconventional message of repentance (John 1:35–42). John was among the many disciples who were captivated by the Baptist. New Testament scholar D. A. Carson describes his ministry:

> [John] resembled the Old Testament prophets who sought to call out a holy remnant from the descendants of Abraham, and anticipated Jesus' insistence that his messianic community would transcend the barriers of race and depend on *personal* faith and new birth.[2]

Ultimately, it would be the one to whom the Baptizer pointed who caught John's attention. One day the wilderness prophet pointed to Jesus and said, "Behold, the Lamb of God, who takes away the sin of the world" (John 1:29 esv), and thus John began listening to the teaching of this itinerant rabbi from Nazareth.

John and the others who were intrigued didn't know then that Jesus would have a plan for them to be more than mere bystanders. John didn't know that, the day he left the Baptizer's entourage and went to listen to this new teacher, he would be part of history, of

God's eternal, redemptive plan to save His people. He couldn't have comprehended what he was signing up for by taking those first, few casual steps toward Jesus.

This rabbi was no ordinary teacher. One day He showed up on the beach, in the middle of a workday, while they were mending their nets for what they assumed would be another day at sea. (Matt. 4:18–22; Mark 1:16–20). We know from the Bible that this is often how God comes to us. For Abraham, it was on an ordinary day in Ur. For Moses, during another run with the sheep on the backside of nowhere. For Paul, on a routine trip to Damascus. You might have your own story of conversion, where God came to you in an otherwise unremarkable conversation with a friend, or after a game in the locker room or in the middle of a shift in a busy restaurant. Or just sitting alone, wondering where your life is going. But He comes. *Follow Me . . .*

We know today what it means to be "fishers of men." We've sung it as kids and have seen the flannelgraph in Sunday school or VBS. But for Jesus this was more than just a clever play on words. Of course, He was using maritime language for those who had spent their lives on the water, but He was doing more than that. Jesus is reaching back to the story of the people of God. As faithful Jews, they would understand that this is the language of the prophets who communicated God's call to His people to righteousness and judgment and repentance. They would be familiar with the divine call in Jeremiah: "'I am about to send for many fishermen'—this is the Lord's declaration—'and they will fish for them'" (Jer. 16:16).

Jesus' call to be "fishers of men" was a seamless sequel to John's message of repentance and coming judgment. Jesus is announcing that the kingdom of God has dawned and that the Son of Man is now calling disciples to declare the message of salvation. Scholar William Lane says that "the summons to be fishers of men is a call to the eschatological task of gathering men in view of the forthcoming judgment of God."[3]

✦ Everything ✦

Let's stop and consider what Jesus is asking of John here. This was not only a decision about his livelihood and future. It was a call to break from his most important community: his family. To leave father and mother behind and follow Jesus would be to give up everything he had ever known.

Sure, he'd seen Jesus perform miracles already. He'd seen friends healed, demons exorcised, and the blind given back their vision, but Jesus is now making a personal ask: to choose the kingdom of God rather than the security of his comfortable life in Capernaum.

Jesus was asking, well, everything. John would hear Jesus say, "If anyone comes to me and does not hate his own father and mother, wife and children, brothers and sisters—yes, and even his own life—he cannot be my disciple" (Luke 14:26). Even in the twenty-first century, when family ties are not as binding as they were in the first, this seems extreme. Today we like to be near Jesus, to take notes as He teaches and marvel at His miracles, but we'd rather He leave us with our nets and our safe way of life. We like a Jesus who forms Himself around our comforts.

But following Him is costly. In the words of J. C. Ryle: "It does cost something to be a real Christian, according to the standard of the Bible. There are enemies to be overcome, battles to be fought, sacrifices to be made, an Egypt to be forsaken, a wilderness to be passed through, a cross to be carried, a race to be run."

At first, to pull James and John from their parents would seem to violate the law of God that Jesus came to fulfill, to break the commandment to "honor your father and your mother." Yet what the kingdom of God demands is not neglect of family and estrangement from loved ones. God is the One who designed the family unit as a beautiful signpost of Christ's relationship with the church. No, what Jesus is asking is deeper. He was wrenching John away from and He's wrenching us away from an idolatry of our family, of holding our loved ones so tight we make the mistake of worshiping them, which isn't good for them, isn't good for us, and doesn't glorify God. And we know that the brothers left the work in the hands of hired help in the Zebedee fishing enterprise, so they took care of their obligations before embarking on this journey with Jesus (Mark 1:20).

We should also not fail to see that John couldn't have gone if Zebedee hadn't first released his son and blessed this call of God upon his life. Patriarchs didn't give up their sons easily in those days. Scholars N. T. Wright and Michael Bird write that "families were extended household entities . . . the household head, *paterfamilias* was the ultimate source of power and identity for the household, and largely determined the social, economic, and religious activities of the family."[4]

Notice how often James and John are described in the gospels as "the sons of Zebedee." Zebedee could have kicked up a fight and held his young apprentice sons tight, refusing to let them go. Instead, the wise father had to have his own moment of following Jesus. He is an example for every father and mother, torn often between our closely held dreams for our children and the mission of God for their lives.

It's easy, of course, for me to write this. My oldest child is fifteen. Right now she's home, though soon I will be handing over the keys to a car and not long after that I'll be sending her to college and perhaps someday I'll be walking her down the aisle or seeing her move to another state or perhaps another country. I'm already feeling it as I write these words. I don't like letting my kids go. Every parent feels the tension, the weight, the gradual pulling away. But somewhere in that moment between Jesus' words and John's response, Zebedee decided to not fight God, to let loose of his own desire for his two sons and let them walk into the wild with Jesus. In an instant, he had to trust that the Son of God cared more for his sons than he did.

And this would be a costly choice. John lived a long life, outliving every other Apostle, writing a gospel, three letters and the book of Revelation—more ink in the New Testament than any other writer. But Zebedee's son James would die a martyr's death, felled by Herod's sword, punished for being a "fisher of men."

Zebedee and his wife, Salome, seemed to embrace the risk of Jesus. Their sons' ministry became their ministry. We see them present at various points in the gospel narrative. Salome makes a rather bold motherly request of Jesus (more on that later) and is there with the other women at Jesus' empty tomb.

Obeying the voice of God seemed to be a family value, an instinctive trait. John, upon hearing Jesus' words, didn't delay or navel gaze or read ten books about finding God's will. The text in Mark and Matthew says John *immediately* went.

✦ Not Ready for Spiritual Leadership ✦

What an act of courage it was for John to leave everything and follow Jesus! And yet, when John became a disciple, he was far from ready for spiritual leadership. This is a reminder that Jesus didn't choose His disciples because of their impressive résumés. I like what one commentator says about Jesus' inner circle: "They showed little potential even for dependability, much less for greatness."[5] Yikes, imagine that written in your high school yearbook.

Jesus, in choosing John, bypassed the traditional places rabbis found their protégés. Jesus chose rough, unpolished young men who possessed only one qualification: they answered yes.

We know Peter's reputation for impulsiveness, but it was actually John who earned the most unflattering nickname from Jesus: "Son of Thunder." Normally, the names Jesus gave meant something profound, a kind of window into someone's future. But with John, this new moniker was a window into his present. It was a not-so-subtle reminder of John's least desirable traits: hot temper and a tendency toward harsh legalism. The church leader most known for his love started out as a self-righteous scold.

Jesus chose rough, unpolished young men who possessed only one qualification: they answered yes.

The gospels have several examples of this on display. Once, John ran breathlessly to Jesus with allegations of counterfeit ministry (Mark 9; Luke 9). It seems someone else in some other place was doing gospel ministry in Jesus' name that wasn't officially sanctioned by the inner circle. John was ready to write that cease-and-desist letter to protect the brand. But Jesus rebuked John and said to him that "whoever is not against you is for you" (Luke 9:50). Of course Jesus was concerned about false teaching and repeatedly warned of wolves among the sheep (Matt. 7:15). But Jesus also could see the false teaching in John's own heart. To this young guardian of the gate, this other group was competition, a siphoning off of the spiritual market share. Apparently, he hadn't quite listened back when John the Baptist, when asked about disciples leaving him and joining Jesus, said "He [Jesus] must increase, but I must decrease" (John 3:30).

This Son of Thunder was less interested in purity and more interested in power. This temptation has beguiled Christians in every age. The future Apostle of Love had a lot to learn. I like what Warren Wiersbe says: "Believers who think that their group is the only group God recognizes and blesses are in for a shock when they get to heaven."[6]

It's not surprising that this episode happened when John and James cornered Jesus with an idea: Master, in the future kingdom, could we flank You, one on the right and one on the left? Matthew's gospel offers a bit more detail, writing that it was Salome, their mother, who first approached Jesus (Matt. 20:20–22). We don't know if there were two moments like this or if Mark, in his more succinct account, cut to the chase and let us know that while Salome was asking, it was really a scheme cooked up by her two ambitious sons.

And if, as many scholars believe, Salome was Mary's sister, this makes the sons' request all the more interesting. Were they attempting to play on family sentiment, using their mother to play on Jesus' affection for His mother to grease the wheels for a promotion?

What we do know is that the two brothers weren't content with being part of the "Peter, James, and John" triumvirate who experienced more of Jesus than any of the other disciples. Jesus had just finished revealing to them His special future mission for them. In the kingdom, they'd "sit on twelve thrones, judging the twelve tribes of Israel" (Matt. 19:28). They would be part of the foundation, along with the Old Testament prophets, upon which the church would be built (Eph. 2:20). But this wasn't enough. They wanted more. The brothers wanted a higher position, a different title, a seat closer to the inner ring of power. Perhaps their eyes were still misty-eyed from the scene they witnessed at the Mount of Transfiguration where Jesus had appeared in glory with Moses and Elijah on either side. Was this James and John signing up to be the next Moses and the new Elijah?

It was a baldly selfish request, one that really angered the other disciples. Though it seems James and John weren't the only ambitious ones. Position and power was a hot topic on those long walks and late nights (Matt. 18:1–4; Mark 9:33–36; Luke 9:46–47). Yet all of this talk about greatness and titles is so incongruent with what Jesus was actually saying about the kingdom of God.

Jesus had just finished explaining what the road to glory would look like for Him. He would be arrested unjustly, endure suffering and crucifixion, and rise again. It's like they fast-forwarded through this teaching and skipped ahead to the part where they'd be ruling on twelve thrones. Jesus answered John and James's question with a question of His own, one in which you can almost hear the sarcasm in His voice: "You don't know what you're asking. Are you able to drink the cup I drink or to be baptized with the baptism I am baptized with?" (Mark 10:38). It's not unlike a response I often give to my eleven-year-old son when he does something foolish: *Are you serious?*

They were dead serious. Of course they could handle it. They'd just climbed a mountain and saw Jesus and Elijah and Moses together.

They'd been with Jesus as He fed the five thousand, walked on water, and healed the sick. Didn't Lazarus just rise from the grave? This was getting fun. How hard could it be to handle being Jesus' wingmen?

James and John were affected with a malady that hurts a lot of young Christian leaders. They were young and self-assured. A lot of good things had happened in the last three years of ministry, so now they thought they knew everything. They thought they were invincible.

> How hard could it be to handle being Jesus' wingmen?

I know this disease because I've suffered from it. I've sat around conference tables and have stood in green rooms with young, cocky leaders seemingly on top of the world. But what John didn't understand in this moment, what most of us don't understand, is that Jesus' pathway to glory wound through suffering and sacrifice.

The cup Jesus would take—that nobody else could endure—was the cup of God's wrath. The disciples would see a glimpse of this when they accompanied Him to the Garden of Gethsemane and saw Him emerge from a time of prayer, sweating drops of blood. The cup John thought he could endure in order to follow Jesus to glory was the one Jesus Himself begged the Father to take away (Matt. 26:39). What's more, their foolish bravado in saying "I can" is the response of every religious person who thinks they can earn their way to God's favor. The truth is, John couldn't bear that cup. You can't bear that cup. Only Jesus could bear that cup and thankfully, in His moment of agony in the garden, Jesus would say, "Yet not as I will, but as you will." He took the cup so we wouldn't have to.

But Jesus was also teaching the disciples that because of His life, death, and resurrection, they'd be able to endure *their* own smaller cups of suffering. This is the new way of leadership in God's counter-cultural kingdom: the way to greatness runs through trails infested by thorns and pain; the way to greatness is self-sacrifice and selflessness. This isn't about intentional self-harm, but a denial of self, made possible only by Jesus' victory over sin and empowered by the Holy Spirit. The two brothers would learn this. James would lose his life, and John would endure the social stigma and persecution of the church in the first century, seeing his family and friends felled by Nero's sword. He would eventually be exiled to the remote island of Patmos.

It is still shocking for us to read, two thousand years later, the audacity of John's request for a prominent place in Jesus' kingdom. It seems so pushy, even rude. Today, if this conversation leaked out, it would be widely mocked on social media and by late-night comics. And yet we engage in the same kind of jockeying for power, if in more subtle, quiet, acceptable ways.

What's interesting is that Jesus didn't actually rebuke them for their desire to be close to Him or even for their desire for greatness. Instead, He explained to them the new way success would be measured. The kingdom of God has a different set of metrics. The way up is now down, the way to power is through giving it up, the path to glory is through service and self-sacrifice. God would raise Jesus from the grave and would exalt Him and give Him "the name that is above every name" (Phil. 2:9).

John's mistake wasn't that he aimed too high with his ambition, but that he set his sights far too low. What John wanted—a temporal earthly position in a short-lived revolution—pales in comparison to what Jesus wanted for him. This is always the temptation of one who follows Jesus—to substitute the fleeting, the cheap, the earthbound, for the greater reward in heaven. And those of us who are built on the foundation of the Apostles will also one day rule in God's final, consummated kingdom when Jesus returns in glory.

✦ A Dinner That Transformed a Disciple ✦

So how did the Son of Thunder become an Apostle of Love? When we open the Bible and read the letters of John, it is hard to imagine that we are reading the words of a legalistic, self-righteous young man. In the early days, John was known more for his legalism than his love. And no one bore the brunt of his lack of grace than the people group every faithful Jew despised: the Samaritans. For one, Samaritans were heretics. They worshiped on the wrong mountain. They didn't accept the full canon of Scripture, only the first five Books of Moses. Oh, and they intermarried with Gentiles who settled in Samaria during the exile. And according to Luke 9, the antipathy was mutual. When Jesus sent ahead a group of disciples to see if they could stay there on the way to Jerusalem, they were rejected. So John did what a Son of Thunder does. He asked Jesus, rather casually, if the Master wanted him (John) to take care of these recalcitrant folks, once and for all.

I like the way the text in Luke records John's words: "Do you want *us* to call down fire . . ." (Luke 9:54, emphasis added). In other words, "Jesus, I can make this problem go away." Here is John again with a bit of an Elijah complex. Fresh off of seeing the prophet at the Transfiguration, he sees himself in that same role. He looked in the mirror and all he saw was himself as the good guy in the epic confrontation with the prophets of Baal on Mt. Carmel (1 Kings 18). This action makes sense too, if you are angling to be Jesus' right-hand man in the kingdom, a sort of Secretary of Defense in the coming revolution. It sure would be nice to take care of these heretics once and for all.

But Jesus didn't indulge John's fantasies. Instead, He rebuked the Son of Thunder. We don't know what was said here, but perhaps Jesus refreshed His friend's memory. Did John so soon forget Jesus' encounter with the woman at the well? The *Samaritan* woman who had a trail of broken relationships and a heretical belief system? Jesus intentionally passed through her part of town, not so He could bring down hellfire on a lost soul but so He could bring her living water.

In this moment, John couldn't see Samaritans or any other people the way Jesus saw them. John saw sinners. Jesus did too, but Jesus saw future citizens of the kingdom of God. Jesus' mission to seek and save the lost didn't just mean lost Jewish people, but the lost from every nation, tribe, and tongue. Jesus even had the audacity to cast a Samaritan, a despised member of the out-group, as a hero in a story about a victim of violence (Luke 10:25–37).

Perhaps Jesus' rebuke was ringing in John's ears still as they made their way into Jerusalem and on toward that fateful week that would change all of their lives forever. In John's life, it seems that the last scene in the Upper Room would be the dawn of a new disciple where the Son of Thunder would become an Apostle of Love.

John and the other disciples assumed this meal, in a rented upstairs room in the old city of Jerusalem, was just another Passover, the annual spiritual and religious ritual where Jews all over the world reflected on God's miraculous rescue from the Egyptians. What they couldn't yet understand was that the blood splattered on Jewish doorposts so long ago was a mere signpost to the shedding of Jesus' blood, splattered across the doorposts of their hearts and an invitation to escape death and find eternal life.

But as they listened to the Master's words that night, they began to understand. The gathering in the Upper Room was likely etched in the memories of every Apostle in the room, but it seems it had an especially profound effect on John. John gives us the lengthiest record of Jesus' words here, in some of the richest passages of Scripture in the entire Bible: John 13–17. This was Jesus' final will and testament: a sobering prediction of His future arrest, of betrayal by one of them, and of God's future presence in them in establishing the church.

Jewish people had adopted the Roman custom of eating while reclining, head toward the table, resting against the left hand while the right hand was used for eating. John, then, did get a place on Jesus' right hand after all, but this was a proximity to a new kind of power. He saw the strength in self-sacrifice as Jesus picked up the basin and towel and slowly washed each of the disciples' dirty, dusty feet. Jesus predicted a future kingdom that would not march through the streets of Jerusalem in victory over the Romans, but away from power toward an ugly instrument of execution and torture.

But the words that most shook John and the others were these: "One of you will betray me" (John 13:21). The disciples couldn't imagine this. Who would betray Jesus? They loved Him. They'd given up everything to follow Him. Like Peter, John believed Jesus was the Christ and knew there was nowhere else to go for the words of eternal life (John 6:68).

As soon as Jesus' words escaped His mouth, John and Peter gave each other knowing glances. Longtime friends and business partners, these two knew each other's body language. So Peter murmured to

Jesus, "Who is it?" to which He said, "He's the one I give the piece of bread to after I have dipped it." Jesus broke off a piece and gave it to Judas and both Peter and John reclined motionless, stunned. *How could it be?*

This experience must have changed John's perspective. This was a different kind of leadership and a different kind of kingdom. Jesus had just washed the feet of the one who sold Him out. He was submitting, not resisting, to the forces that were bringing Him down. As if the unjust arrest, the whispered conspiracies, the skullduggery of His opponents was all part of some grand plan—the Father's plan.

It is in the Upper Room where John is first referred to as "the disciple whom Jesus loved."

This is where following Jesus took John. A place at Jesus' right hand meant not calling down fire from heaven but calling up love, Calvary's love, for those far from God. It is interesting that it is in the Upper Room where John is first referred to as "the disciple whom Jesus loved" (ESV).

John's gospel, written decades after the other gospels, is the only one to refer to John this way. John isn't implying that Jesus loved John more than the others. What I believe John is saying is that in this moment he saw, for the first time up close, real otherworldly love, and that nobody at that table, including Judas, needed Jesus' love more than he. Charles Spurgeon is right when he says, "to be loved as John was, with a special love, is an innermost form of that same grace with which all believers have been favoured. . . . He, like all the rest of his brethren, was loved of Jesus because Jesus is all love, and chose to set his heart upon him."[7]

I think it was in the Upper Room where John began to shed his worldly ambitions. A Son of Thunder may have entered that rented space, but a new Apostle emerged. Writing in his gospel years later, John could only revel in God's love for him. And in his letter to the church, he'd write these words:

> *See what great love the Father has given us that we should be called God's children—and we are! The reason the world does not know us is that it didn't know him. (1 John 3:1)*

✦ **At the Foot of the Cross** ✦

John's transformation in the Upper Room is why, I believe, we find him at the foot of the cross when everyone else had scattered. The rest of the disciples fled in fear. Peter denied Jesus. But here is John, with Jesus' mother in the last moments of Jesus' life.

It's easy for us to sentimentalize the cross today, even on Good Friday. We are so far removed from the reality of the bloody scene on that hillside outside Jerusalem. People walked by and mocked them. Others watched the spectacle of disgraced outcasts get their due. Soldiers gambled and waited for the prisoners to die so they could finish their shift.

What horror John must have witnessed that dark day. This was his best friend, beaten beyond recognition, body lashed open, nails penetrating His hands and feet, lungs struggling to gather oxygen. There is no way to sanitize what John saw.

How John must have wept in anguish as Jesus cried out to the Father, "Why have you forsaken me?" (Matt. 27:46 ESV). What must John have felt as the sun darkened and the earth split open and as Jesus shouted those final words: "It is finished"? The thought must have occurred to John: *It's true. Only Jesus could take this cup.*

And yet even in His final hours Jesus had a kind word for John, the one who had so often been foolish and misunderstanding. "Behold, your mother!" Jesus said to John through labored breathing, and to Mary, "Woman, behold, your son!" (John 19:26–27 ESV). This was Jesus entrusting His most treasured earthly relationship to the care of His best friend.

But it was more than Jesus fulfilling the command to honor His mother. Jesus was also inviting John into a new kind of family, one that transcends even our earthly alliances. This is how disciples can leave "father and mother and sister and brother" to follow Jesus. At the foot of Christ's cross, we gain new sisters and brothers, new mothers and new fathers. And what a joy it is to be received into the worldwide fellowship of saints, in heaven and on earth and around the world, not based on our family status or lineage, but because we have God's seal of approval and Christ's blood stamped on our spiritual birth certificate.

Jesus was inviting John into a new kind of family.

I imagine it is here, in the darkest moment in human history, when the Son of God gasped for air, when blood ran down His body, when the shame and humiliation of the worst kinds of evil rested on Jesus, where John first had the words to write what would become Holy Spirit–inspired Scripture about the gospel he would spend his life proclaiming:

> *What was from the beginning, what we have heard, what we have seen with our eyes, what we have observed and have touched with our hands, concerning the word of life—that life was revealed, and we have seen it and we testify and declare to you the eternal life that was with the Father and was revealed to us—what we have seen*

and heard we also declare to you, so that you may also have fellow-ship with us; and indeed our fellowship is with the Father and with his Son, Jesus Christ. (1 John 1:1–4)

✦ Outrunning Peter ✦

Where did John go after Jesus' body was taken down from the cross and given to Joseph of Arimathea for burial? Did he stay by the grieving Mary's side? The next time we see him, he's with Peter the following Sunday morning. Was it here that Peter confided to John about his denial on the night of Jesus' arrest? We do know that whatever they were doing was interrupted by Mary Magdalene reporting on what she and the other women had just seen. Years later, John would record this in his gospel, the memories undoubtedly fresh and vivid:

> *So she ran and went to Simon Peter and the other disciple, the one whom Jesus loved, and said to them, "They have taken the Lord out of the tomb, and we do not know where they have laid him." So Peter went out with the other disciple, and they were going toward the tomb. Both of them were running together, but the other disciple outran Peter and reached the tomb first. And stooping to look in, he saw the linen cloths lying there, but he did not go in. Then Simon Peter came, following him, and went into the tomb. He saw the linen cloths lying there, and the face cloth, which had been on Jesus' head, not lying with the linen cloths but folded up in a place by itself. Then the other disciple, who had reached the tomb first, also went in, and he saw and believed. (John 20:2–8 ESV)*

I have read this passage of Scripture every Easter of my life, and yet I still find John's words beautiful and fascinating. It makes sense that in this resurrection scene, he describes himself as the disciple "whom Jesus loved." The horrific execution he had just witnessed and the empty tomb before him were symbols of Jesus' love. It's also interesting that he added in the detail that he "outran Peter"—a little shade perhaps? It was after all Peter, speaking through Mark's pen, who saw fit to mention that Jesus nicknamed John "Son of Thunder" (Mark 3:17). Or maybe it was just a detail that stuck in his mind. *I remember that day. Running as fast as I could toward Joseph's tomb, and I got there before Peter.* But he would allow Peter to enter the tomb first, before John stooped and saw and believed.

He saw and believed. Perhaps in this moment he remembered Jesus' words to Mary and Martha about Lazarus, that Jesus Himself was "the resurrection and the life" (John 11:25), or perhaps the teaching in the Upper Room was coming back into focus. But seeing the wide-open grave, the folded clothes in Peter's hands, John believed.

Like Peter, he couldn't know what all this would mean for his future. He hadn't fully fleshed out the reality of the resurrection of the Son of God, but he knew enough to know this: The One he loved, who loved him, was alive.

John would see Jesus several more times in the coming days. Twice in appearances in that same Upper Room, and on the shores of Galilee as Jesus once again renewed His call to Peter and the other Apostles. He would hear Jesus' teaching to go and make more disciples. He would stand there as Jesus ascended into heaven before Pentecost. John, more than the others, would chronicle the physical nature of Jesus' post-resurrection life, the nail scars in His hands, the food on the table in the room and on the beach near the Sea of Galilee. We know he included this to fend off the Gnostics who would later come and say that Jesus was not fully human. But John knew that Jesus' resurrection was a physical, bodily resurrection. And he would come to see Christ's resurrection power blow through this formerly cowardly, unlearned, brash group of men and turn the world upside down. This movement would explode out of Jerusalem and Galilee and across the entire known world.

Most of all, John would see, in his own life, the powerful impact of the Spirit's work. He would write the Gospel of John, perhaps the most read book of the Bible, a go-to section that has turned many skeptics into saints. He would pen three letters to the church, mixing admonitions against sin with pastoral notes of compassion and nurture. He would be tasked with writing about the end of the age in a vision we call Revelation, or, sometimes, the Revelation of John.

Church tradition has it that John died of old age around AD 100. Besides writing more of the New Testament than any other human author, he became a wise elder to the church at Ephesus, cared for Jesus' mother, influenced the next generation of the church, including two great leaders: Ignatius, the bishop of Antioch, and Polycarp, the bishop of Smyrna, who at his trial refused to recant the faith, saying famously: "[Eighty-six] years have I served Christ, and He hath never done me wrong; how then can I now blaspheme my King and Saviour?"[8]

But the greatest work of God in John's life was that the one-time Son of Thunder, who wished to extinguish his political enemies with fire, became known for a different kind of power. Love would become a major theme of his apostolic ministry (1 John 3:14–20; 4:7–21; 5:1; 2 John 6).

We know that we have passed from death to life because we love our brothers and sisters. The one who does not love remains in death.

Everyone who hates his brother or sister is a murderer, and you know
that no murderer has eternal life residing in him. This is how we
have come to know love: He laid down his life for us. We should also
lay down our lives for our brothers and sisters. (1 John 3:14–16)

The love John saw at Easter fueled his own love. The one who witnessed Jesus lay down His life was now willing to lay it down for his brothers and sisters. The mark that one has had a true encounter with the living Christ is the willingness to demonstrate otherworldly love.

Study Questions:

Trace John's early life and journey with Jesus.

◆ What about Jesus might have compelled him to leave behind his familiar life as a fisherman and follow this itinerant rabbi into an unknown future?

◆ What passions fueled John's desire to crush anyone who opposed him and punish others doing ministry?

◆ What characteristics might you see in your own life that might qualify you as a "Son of Thunder" or "Daughter of Thunder"?

◆ Follow John's later life with Jesus, at the foot of the cross and at the resurrection:

  ◆ What changed in John's attitude and disposition?
  ◆ Why did Jesus entrust the care of His mother to John?
  ◆ How did Jesus' resurrection power change this Son of Thunder into an Apostle of Love?

Suggested Hymns and Songs:

The Power of the Cross—Stuart Townend
The Love of God—Frederick Lehman

CHAPTER THREE

The Betrayer

Judas

His life was the antithesis of love.[1]

MERRILL C. TENNEY

*"Brothers and sisters, it was necessary that the Scripture be fulfilled
that the Holy Spirit through the mouth of David foretold about
Judas, who became a guide to those who arrested Jesus. For he was
one of our number and shared in this ministry."*

ACTS 1:16–17

He was a decorated soldier, known for his daring exploits in winning battles for the ragtag band of doctors and lawyers and farmers taking on the mighty British army. Had the Revolutionary War ended in the spring of 1780, we might remember Benedict Arnold for his exploits on behalf of the Continental Army. But intercepted messages delivered to General George Washington just before a planned breakfast with Arnold's family on the banks of the Hudson River revealed the shocking truth: The soldier who had risked his life for the Americans was flipping to the British side.

You don't even have to be an American history nerd to cringe when hearing Benedict Arnold's name. Desperate for money, he sold himself to the British army for the equivalent of $3 million. Today his name is synonymous with betrayal. Yet as much as Americans loathe Arnold, he will only ever come a distant second as history's most despised turncoat.

Only one figure in human history has a more ignominious name than Benedict Arnold: Judas Iscariot. He's been a favorite of artists ranging from Dante's assigning Judas to the lowest circle of hell, gnawed on forever by a demon with three heads, to Metallica's iconic song "Judas Kiss." He has made appearances in old English ballads and in Lady Gaga songs.

For Christians, we understand that Judas's story is at the center of the Easter story. You cannot enter the Lenten season, break bread on Maundy Thursday, mourn on Good Friday, or rejoice on Resurrection Sunday without first passing through the still-shocking, hard-to-believe but true story of Judas Iscariot and his betrayal of Jesus.

✦   Judas, Gospel Preacher   ✦

Before Judas descended into infamy, he was a disciple of Jesus Christ, an Apostle, one of the twelve men chosen as part of Jesus' earthly ministry.

It's hard to get Judas's kiss of betrayal out of our heads and it's hard to un-see his hands clasped around a bag of silver coins as he's leaving the temple treasury. But if you parachuted into first-century Israel and interviewed the people who knew the most about Jesus of Nazareth, sat down with Jesus' closest friends and family, and queried the critics, you would hear from them that one of the most loyal, devoted, gifted men in this Jesus movement was Judas, son of Simon.

We don't know when Jesus called Judas or the circumstances around it. We don't know when the Judean first laid eyes on the Galilean preacher, the unconventional rabbinic revolutionary from Nazareth. But what we do know is that he left whatever he was doing in his previous life to follow Jesus. We gloss over this as we read the gospel narratives, as if to be a disciple in those days was as simple as a twice-a-month visit to an air-conditioned building and the lip-syncing of a few worship songs. But to follow Jesus in the first century was a radical move, something only those on the devoted fringe were willing to do. Sure, Jesus drew crowds at times, swelling after He fed the thousands on the hillsides or healed the lame and the sick. But the crowds were fickle and also left when He spoke hard things (John 6:60). Yet Judas didn't walk away then, didn't abandon Christ.

Judas, for three years (imagine spending three years of your life doing anything), was locked in. And it's not like he was just a spectator; he, like the other disciples, was empowered by Jesus for a unique apostolic gospel ministry:

> *Summoning the Twelve, he gave them power and authority over all the demons and to heal diseases. Then he sent them to proclaim the kingdom of God and to heal the sick. (Luke 9:1–2)*

Think about this. Judas Iscariot, yes, that Judas Iscariot, "proclaimed the kingdom of God" and healed the sick. There were people, many perhaps, whose hearts turned toward Christ because of Judas's preaching and whose sicknesses were healed by his hand. What's more, imagine what Judas saw in his three years side by side with Jesus. He witnessed Jesus still a raging sea with His words. He saw disabled men and women walk, the blind find sight, the demon-possessed find freedom. Judas participated in the miracle where Jesus took a little boy's lunch and turned it into a buffet for a stadium full of hungry people. Judas was there when a decomposing corpse named Lazarus shook off his grave clothes and came stumbling out of a cheap tomb. He saw Jesus give eternal life to the woman at the well, listened to Jesus preach in the synagogues, heard Him deliver the Sermon on the Mount.

Judas saw all of this, live. Participated in it. He *did* ministry in the name of Jesus. Judas was a gospel preacher. Writing about this, pastor Colin Smith says, "Judas walked with Jesus for three years. He saw the greatest life ever lived up close and personal. You can't have a better model of faith than Jesus or a better environment for forming faith than Judas had in walking with the Savior."[2]

It's hard to fathom. If you knew Judas, if you bumped into him in the market in Hebron or were in the crowd gathered as Jesus taught on the shores of Galilee or caught a glimpse of Judas as he accompanied Jesus to the temple, you'd be convinced, in your mind, that there were few people on the planet as sold out, as all-in, as committed to the kingdom of God as Judas. And so did Jesus' inner circle. So much so they made Judas the treasurer, the one who managed the books and collected the money for their fledgling movement.

Judas was loved, gifted, *sacrificial*. We will get to the betrayal, but we must first see Judas as the friend, the fellow Apostle, the devoted follower of Jesus. "My close friend," King David wrote centuries earlier in a foreshadowing of later betrayal of a future Son of David, " . . . has turned against me" (Ps. 41:9 NIV).

✦ Why, Judas, Why? ✦

So why did Judas do it? This is the question we have asked for two thousand years. There exists no shortage of theories and conspiracies as playwrights and novelists and filmmakers have used creative license to divine Judas's motives. A medieval fable has Judas betraying Jesus because of a wicked sister. A novel, *I Judas*, makes the case for Judas being tricked by Zerah, a temple scribe. And of course we have the *Last Temptation of Christ*, the Martin Scorsese film based on the 1960s-era Nikos Kazantzakis novel, which portrays Judas in a sympathetic light, with the betrayal plot a means to force Jesus' admission of deity and begin His conquest of Rome. Not to mention *Jesus Christ Superstar* and a thousand other creative offerings.

The truth is that we don't know fully what motivated Judas to turn on Jesus. And while the betrayal narrative happened in a short sequence of time, Judas's heart turned toward betrayal long before this. Chuck Swindoll reminds us that nobody "suddenly becomes villainous and corrupt. It's a process. It takes time. One step leads to another, which in turn leads the person deeper, which in turn leads the person still deeper, which leads to the act itself that goes down in infamy."[3]

The gospel writers don't give us a lot of information about Judas. You can imagine why they didn't spice up their narratives, years later, with tidbits of the betrayer's life. Writing under the inspiration of the Holy Spirit, who didn't see fit to include a lengthy bio in the canon of Scripture, the Evangelists wrote sparingly of their former friend. There are no anecdotes about Judas or quotes of his interactions with other disciples or with Jesus. He is mentioned in the lists of those Jesus called, though always last. And every mention of him includes the editorial note that this Judas, yes this one, was the one who turned. Reading the gospels, you can almost feel the emotion in Matthew, Mark, Luke, and John as they struggle to write about their former friend.

So we don't know where Judas first met Jesus. We don't know exactly when he gave up everything and decided to follow Jesus. But from what little information we have, we can find some clues to his treachery. First, most scholars believe "Iscariot" is not a last name, but likely refers to the place where Judas grew up, a town named Kerioth, about fifteen miles from Hebron, in southern Judea.

This set him apart from the other eleven disciples, who came from the Galilee region in the north of Israel. Folks from this southern part of the country were less trusting of the Roman government and more supportive of revolution and resistance. However, Judas was not as extreme as the subversive Simon the Zealot, another Apostle.

We know from the gospel of John that Judas loved money.

So was Judas first attracted to Jesus because he thought this new Messiah would lead a resistance to Rome? Was he awed by the miracles because those miracles validated Jesus' kingship and would become a catalyst for a new world order? Did he preach the kingdom of God because he saw it (as did most every disciple) as the vehicle for contemporary political victory and relief from unjust occupation?

We know from the gospel of John that Judas loved money. When Mary of Bethany anoints the feet of Jesus with expensive perfume, it struck Judas as an outrageous waste of resources. But John tells us that Judas cared mostly about the potential for the balance sheet, dreaming of the additional revenue that could have been given toward the movement if Mary had just sold that perfume and dropped the equivalent of an annual salary into the moneybag.

John writes that Judas used the cover of advocacy for the poor as a way of hiding his true intent. Judas, sadly, was not the last religious person to use performative activism, to wield a vulnerable people group as a cudgel against someone else. But was it only money that motivated Judas? Let's not forget that the other gospels record all the disciples sharing his sentiment. This tells us the level of influence he had among the twelve. Trusted enough to mind the books and hold the money pouch, Judas's complaint made fiscal sense. A movement needs money to last, to grow, and wasting it on extravagant displays seemed foolish.

And let's remember how much Judas gave up to be a follower of Jesus. Like the others, he had left whatever career ambitions he had to bet on Jesus, that this miracle-working Messiah was the real deal. So perhaps Judas's motives were mixed: money and power, the two deadly elixirs often combine as a cocktail for evil in the hearts of men. It is interesting to me that Matthew and Mark both juxtapose this scene in Bethany with Judas's meeting up with the chief priests and scribes and offering his services to Jesus' enemies.

I think this was the final straw for Judas that finally broke him in a bad way. A revolutionary and a nationalist at heart, he saw Jesus as a vessel for his own political, social, and personal desires. It seems Judas's desire was to buy in early on the Jesus movement, perhaps to be the treasurer in a new earthly kingdom. But the bag kept getting lighter and Jesus was making all the wrong moves for someone who was supposed to build a movement and topple the unjust Roman occupation.

We see this most vividly in John 6. Jesus miraculously feeds thousands of people and His popularity is swelling. If you are Judas, if you are anyone who has left everything to join up with Jesus, this is the moment you are validated in your life choices. This is where it all comes together—and yet we see Jesus do the opposite of what He should be doing. Instead of embracing the crowds and riding the wave into earthly power, He . . . recedes:

**Jesus is
thinning
the crowd,
not adding.**

> *Therefore, when Jesus realized that they were about to come and take him by force to make him king, he withdrew again to the mountain by himself. (John 6:15)*

If you are an activist from a place roiling with revolutionary fervor, this had to be puzzling. Disillusioning. All the blood, sweat, and tears he'd poured out for three years—and Jesus throws it away. But it gets worse. Later in John 6, a day after Jesus walked on water and demonstrated to the disciples His power over creation, the crowds approach Him and ask for another miracle, another showstopping sign from heaven. He refuses and instead offers up what John describes as hard teaching (John 6:60), and even more followers abandon Him. Jesus is thinning the crowd, not adding. He's doing the opposite of what you'd need to do to be the next king of Israel.

And in this moment, Jesus asks the disciples, "You don't want to go away too, do you?" prompting Peter's reply, "Lord, to whom will we go? You have the words of eternal life" (John 6:68). Judas is silent. He stays, like the other eleven, but Jesus' response tells us something, perhaps, about what is going on inside Judas's heart:

Jesus replied to them, "Didn't I choose you, the Twelve? Yet one of you is a devil." He was referring to Judas, Simon Iscariot's son, one of the Twelve, because he was going to betray him. (John 6:70–71)

This is the first time Jesus predicts His betrayal. He knew the seed that was implanted here in Judas's heart. Jesus was refusing the kingdom Judas wanted for Him.

So yes, Judas betrayed Jesus because Judas was greedy—skimming off the top, dismissing the radical generosity of the woman washing Jesus' feet, selling Jesus for thirty pieces of silver. But it was much darker and deeper than a mere wanting of more money. The thirty pieces of silver was a decent sum of money for a day laborer, perhaps four months of pay, but not a life-changing amount for Judas. The price is actually an insult, equivalent to the price the owner of an ox gored to death would be paid as compensation. Judas, enraged about the wasting of one year's salary in devotion to Jesus, sold Him out for far less. Judas's value system was upside down. And betrayal was available at a much cheaper price than the cost of love.

This gospel preacher became an enemy of the cross because he saw Jesus more as a vessel for his own ambitions than a Savior for his soul. Judas was after political revolution. He was after power. In the spilled perfume, he saw no upside, no profit margin. In Jesus' denying those who wanted to make Him king, he saw a foolish, soft mentality. In the disciples, he saw easy marks whose money he could take without them knowing. Everything was about winning and losing. He saw the world in black-and-white terms: Those who know how to play the game, and those who don't. Jesus didn't play this game. The first would be last, He said. The kingdom of God that Jesus talked about was a rebuke to Judas's Darwinian worldview.

And by the end, Jesus was no longer a useful revolutionary, but a liability to the revolution that needed to happen, the wrong kind of Messiah. So Judas cashed out, cut his losses, and moved on. The theologian Karl Barth says in such a poignant way about Judas: "He is not opposed to Jesus. He even wishes to be for Him. But he is for Him in such a way—not totally, that is to say—that actually he is against Him."[4]

It's hard to believe that the one who saw Jesus up close, who preached salvation and whose hands brought healing, could turn on the One who called him. And yet looking back it might not be that surprising. Even in the words we see Judas use to describe Jesus: You will notice in the gospels he never calls Jesus "Lord." In Matthew, when he asks Jesus, "Surely not I, *Rabbi*" (Matt. 26:25). In the garden at Jesus' arrest, all the gospels have him addressing Jesus as "teacher." Never Lord. Contrast this with Thomas touching the resurrected Jesus, exclaiming, "My Lord and my God!" (John 20:28). Or the disciples asking about their possibility of betrayal, saying "Is it, I Lord?"

> You will notice in the gospels Judas never calls Jesus "Lord."

But not Judas. Church father Jerome says this is significant. "He who was the traitor did not call him Lord but teacher, as if to have an excuse, upon rejecting the Lord, for having betrayed at most a teacher."[5] And thus we see someone so very *close* to Jesus, who did "many wonderful things" in Jesus' name, who was familiar with the Jesus language and experienced in the Jesus movement, but never made Jesus Lord.

What a sad indictment. And this, I'm afraid, is the situation for many who celebrate Easter this and every year. A familiarity with the language, dressing up for the occasion, even brought to tears by Jesus' death and resurrection. But never able to call Jesus "Lord."

Jesus, as you know, is still quite popular today, but is it the Jesus who demands we take up a cross, who promises suffering, who isn't content with being one of many options but demands our worship? The truth is, while we easily loathe Judas on Easter, we are far more like the betrayer than we would like to admit. We are too easily tempted to see Jesus as a vessel for our aspirations than as the Lord of our lives, the one worthy of worship and adoration and praise. And if we were honest, we'd admit to selling out Jesus for far less than thirty pieces of silver.

✦ What Judas Tells Us About Jesus ✦

But Judas's story is not really about Judas at all. The story is about Jesus. I'm captivated by the scene in the Upper Room the night of Jesus' arrest. Jesus knew He would be betrayed by the one He loved and yet demonstrates a divine, hard-to-believe love toward His enemy. Today we, like so many—maybe most—before us grapple with His command to "love your enemies, do what is good to those who hate you" (Luke 6:27). But perhaps we'd fully understand the implications of this if we contemplated more of Jesus' interactions with His betrayer.

The scene opens with Jesus' washing of the disciples' feet before the Passover meal. Many speculate that because this was a private meal, the usual servants or dinner help at a meal like this were not present. Nobody stepped up to wash feet, so Jesus reached down with the towel and washed the feet of the Twelve. This is in the context of the arguments the disciples were having about who would be greatest in the kingdom of God. Jesus, they thought, would show them who was greatest in the kingdom. We typically read this part of the Easter story and focus on Peter's interaction with Jesus, refusing to have his feet washed by his Master. But we forget that waiting in line for his footwashing was Judas. Jesus didn't bypass His betrayer in disgust, letting him approach the table with dirty feet. He took out the towel and the basin and gently wiped the dirty toes of the one who had already accepted money for Jesus' arrest.

It's an unfathomable, otherworldly kind of love. It reminds us that divine love is really always one way. "We love because he first loved us" (1 John 4:19). Later Paul, the chief of sinners, would say, "While we were still sinners, Christ died for us" (Rom. 5:8). And Jesus loved him up until the moment of Jesus' arrest and beyond that moment. As they gathered at the table, Judas seemed to sit close to the Master, a place of prominence and intimacy. We know this because John tells us that when Jesus revealed to Judas that He knew he was the betrayer, nobody else in that room caught the exchange.

✦ Jesus Knew ✦

Jesus knew—and He wasn't surprised. He said, "But behold, the hand of him who betrays me is with me on the table" (Luke 22:21 ESV). The disciples began to argue among themselves about who it might be. Scholar Michael Green writes, "Jesus tells them that he will be betrayed by one who has the closest ties of sacred table fellowship with him. . . . To break that tie was anathema."[6] The breaking of bread in the Middle East, then and now, signifies the idea that "you are my friend and I will not hurt you."[7] Jesus here is approaching Judas in friendship, even as He is confirming his betrayal.

All of the disciples asked Jesus, "Is it I, Lord?"—a genuinely self-searching question. Except for Judas. Matthew has him asking, "Is it I, Rabbi?" He deliberately addressed Jesus as "Rabbi," not "Lord." But not only did Jesus know, He wasn't surprised by Judas's betrayal.

We have to understand that Jesus was not the victim of a nefarious plot, but in control even of His own betrayal and arrest in the garden. Judas's treachery was part of God's long and sure plan of salvation promised way back in Genesis. As one commentator says, Judas was "part of Satan's plan, but God's counterplan."[8] Here Judas, doing the work of the serpent, was nipping at the heels of the seed of the woman, but God was fully in control. Nobody took Jesus' life; Jesus willingly laid it down (John 10:18). The prophets echoed and shadowed this day:

> *"Throw it to the potter," the LORD said to me—this magnificent price I was valued by them. So I took the thirty pieces of silver and threw it into the house of the LORD, to the potter. (Zech. 11:13)*

And King David, speaking of his own betrayal at the hands of a trusted friend, is used by the Spirit of God to offer a shadow of a future son of David who would be betrayed at the hands of a friend:

> *Even my friend in whom I trusted,*
> *one who ate my bread,*
> *has raised his heel against me. (Ps. 41:9)*

It's hard for us to fathom this—how Jesus could be betrayed and yet know ahead of time who His betrayer would be, how God could be in control and yet Judas, with his sinful human heart, willingly commit this evil—but this is what Jesus tells us:

"For the Son of Man will go just as it is written about him, but woe to that man by whom the Son of Man is betrayed! It would have been better for him if he had not been born." (Mark 14:21)

Nothing about what happened to Jesus is accidental; nothing caught the Godhead by surprise; nothing rattled the windows of Heaven. Jesus suffered death, John Calvin said, "not by constraint, but willingly, that he might be a voluntary sacrifice."[9] And yet, Judas was completely responsible for his actions. Once before, a son of Abraham was unjustly sold to his enemies and he too spoke of this paradox. Joseph, facing his brothers who betrayed him, said, "You planned evil against me; God planned it for good to bring about the present result—the survival of many people" (Gen. 50:20). And Peter, standing at Pentecost many days later, would say of the arrest of Jesus:

"Though he was delivered up according to God's determined plan and foreknowledge, you used lawless people to nail him to a cross and kill him." (Acts 2:23)

This tension between God's sovereignty and human responsibility, a mystery Christians still have not fully grasped, should give us confidence this Easter that we are not celebrating a nice story—but a real story. Jesus' foreknowledge of His betrayal and His fulfillment of ancient prophecies validate Easter. It is not just pastel colors and pretty dresses, but the story of God's renewal of His people and His creation, the dawn of a new kingdom.

And yet we ask, did Judas *have* to betray Jesus? Could he have turned his heart toward God and away from evil? Yes, he could have. We see this even in Jesus' use of the strong warning "woe to that man by whom the Son of Man is betrayed!"

When Jesus spoke privately to Judas at the table, William Hull writes, "To Jesus, this simple act represented love's last appeal to one on the verge of perdition." Love's last appeal: the washing of Judas's feet, the sharing of an intimate meal, the strong warnings—all in an attempt to pull Judas away. "To Judas, it may have seemed like a final invitation to accept Jesus' strategy of suffering love, an offer which he rebuffed."[10]

Judas rebuffed Him, and the Bible records that as he left Jesus a final time, Satan indwelt Judas. We forget, too often, that this conflict and every skirmish between good and evil is more than just the humans involved, but part of a cosmic battle, a war between God and Satan. Later Paul wrote, " For we do not wrestle against flesh and blood, but against the rulers, against the authorities, against the cosmic powers over this present darkness, against the spiritual forces of evil in the heavenly places" (Eph. 6:12 esv). This war, at this moment, centered in one man's heart, the heart of Judas. And by rejecting Jesus, he chose the devil.

> There is no neutrality in the war for our souls.

It seems so backward, so medieval to say that someone is "choosing the devil." We are so sophisticated in this age. We believe in science and data and reality. And yet these are the two choices that any human being faces. There is no neutrality in the war for our souls. We will be captive, a disciple, to someone. For Judas, his choice was Satan.

John writes of Judas, "After receiving the piece of bread, he immediately left. And it was night" (John 13:30). It's no coincidence that John writes, "and it was night." There is a stunning contrast between the way of Judas and the way of Jesus. Judas left filled by the devil and met a sad and destructive end. This is always the way of sin. Sin, when it conceives, brings forth death (James 1:15). And there is the way of Jesus, who is the light of the world, who defeated death by His resurrection and ascended into heaven so we could be filled with the Spirit of God. There is the filling with the light of the Spirit or the filling with the darkness of the evil one. Pastor Colin Smith says, "Judas went out into the darkness he had chosen. When you get close to Jesus, one of two things will happen: either you will become wholly his, or you will end up more alienated from him."[11]

At the end, when Judas and the soldiers came, He who formed these soldiers in their mothers' wombs, who breathed the world into existence, yielded quietly and willingly. He could have brought down the fire of Heaven, but instead He chose to accept the kiss of His betrayer and bring salvation to His people. New Testament scholar Thomas Schreiner sums it up well: "Jesus' betrayal occurred just as the Scriptures predicted, and so nothing took place by surprise, though Judas still bore responsibility for his sin. God worked in and through the actions of human beings and so he is the one who struck down Jesus as the shepherd. The cup that Jesus received was from the Father."[12]

✦ How Religion Failed Judas ✦

This is a book about the characters of Easter, but sadly this character, whose betrayal stands at the center of this grand narrative, didn't make it to Resurrection Sunday. His story ends in despair. A guilt-ridden Judas slunk back to his conspiracy cohorts and admits, "I have sinned by betraying innocent blood" (Matt. 27:4).

It's heartwrenching to read the narrative. Overwhelmed by his sin, he returns the thirty pieces of silver. I don't know what turned Judas, what triggered his remorse. It does seem that Judas came to his senses before Jesus' trial even began. We might imagine the weight of his sin sinking down into his soul after the adrenaline of the arrest, when the reality of what he did settled over him as night fell. We do know that he came to the place where his broken soul should have found relief: the religious establishment, the very people who should have represented God to him. And yet those religious leaders could only shrug and say, "What's that to us?" (v. 4).

Judas was failed by the religious system that should have brought him closer to God. It was the religious leaders who first eagerly indulged his desire to cash in on Jesus' revolution. And those same religious leaders had nothing for him when he was at his most despondent, when he could have found repentance and restoration. "What's that to us?" As a result, a soul that could have been restored perished for eternity, seeking his own atonement by hanging himself.

But those leaders took the money. And they bought property with it, a field that was called a "field of blood" (Acts 1:19).

I can't help but wonder: What if Judas had known the same repentance and restoration that Peter did? Both failed Jesus, and yet, while Peter experienced both remorse and redemption, Judas found no such spiritual relief. How tragic. What Judas never realized is that his blood didn't have to soak an empty field, but instead he could have found atonement in the blood of another, the one whom he betrayed. He could have turned to Jesus and found forgiveness of his sin. He could have, like the prodigal son, found forgiveness from the Father. He could have come home.

This Easter, it's helpful for us to remember that we are like Judas in that we too have betrayed Jesus, time and time again. We've sold Him out for lesser idols. But we don't have to suffer Judas's fate. If we confess our sins, He's faithful and just to forgive our sins and cleanse us from all unrighteousness (1 John 1:9). While we were yet sinners, Jesus died for us. Jesus' blood can remove, remit, and erase our sins before a holy God. The One we have betrayed has taken our guilt from us. And we rejoice.

STUDY QUESTIONS:

✦ Consider this statement: "Judas was a gospel preacher." How is it that this seemingly faithful disciple could suddenly turn on Jesus?

✦ Contrast Judas's desire for earthly revolution with Jesus' description of a spiritual kingdom.

✦ What motivations were revealed in Judas's heart when he objected to the expensive gift by Mary of Bethany?

✦ How did the religious establishment fail Judas, both in working with him to betray Jesus and failing to comfort him in his final hours?

SUGGESTED HYMNS AND SONGS:

Nothing But the Blood—Robert Lowry
There Is Power in the Blood—Lewis E. Jones

CHAPTER FOUR

The Rogue

Barabbas

*The criminal escaped; Christ was condemned. The one guilty
of many crimes received a pardon; he who had remitted the crimes
of all who confess was condemned. And yet the cross itself also,
if you reflect upon it, was a courtroom. In the middle of it stood
the final judge.*[1]

Augustine

*For Christ also suffered for sins once for all, the righteous for the
unrighteous, that he might bring you to God. He was put to death
in the flesh but made alive by the Spirit.*

1 Peter 3:18

Have you ever gotten in trouble for something you didn't do?
Alternatively, have you ever done something wrong and gotten
away with it? I can think of two examples from my childhood.

Once I was scheduled to go with our school on a field trip to go
swimming. In the private Christian academy I attended, good behavior and decent grades meant you were able to attend the field trip. If
you got a demerit that week, you were disqualified. Well, I didn't get

a demerit. And on Friday I packed my swimming trunks and was excited about getting on the bus and making the trip to nearby Harper College. Only, I didn't get to go. I wasn't on the list.

I was convinced there was some mistake. So I voiced my opinion, and the teachers and principal didn't budge. I was in fifth grade, so I went home and complained to my parents. My dad, an old-school plumber who grew up in a broken home and had to work to support his family since he was fourteen, had little sympathy. "Yeah, I'm sorry, Son. But this probably makes up for the time you got away with something."

Then there was that time I did get away with something. I'm ashamed even now to write about it, almost thirty years later. But here it is. Every year I volunteered to work at a camp my church owned. We'd clean boats, clean fish, rake beaches, wash bathrooms, work in the kitchen, and a whole lot of other jobs young boys hate but do anyway. Well one day, for some reason, a couple of us were doing what teenage boys seem to do when nobody is watching: playing with fire. Literally. We were messing around with matches and paper and wood. When we were done, I carelessly tossed a twig I had thought was no longer burning into a garbage trailer and went about my business.

About twenty minutes later, our camp director was yelling, "The garbage trailer is on fire!" and he and a few others grabbed buckets of water to put it out. Thankfully it didn't cause much damage to the trailer, but if it had, it could have caught the nearby cabins on fire and turned into a disaster.

What's worse, I never 'fessed up to the crime and nobody knew how it started. Well, until now, if they happen to pick up this Easter book. Jon, I'm so sorry.

When I think back, I still cringe at my duplicity. I should have gotten in trouble for that. And I'm still a little chapped I missed that fifth-grade swimming trip. That would have been fun.

Of course, these are relatively minor incidents I share with my kids and make them laugh. It's much more serious when truly innocent people are arrested and jailed for crimes they didn't commit, or when violent criminals get away with their crimes. At the center of Easter is the story of perhaps the most famous prisoner set free and the most unjust trial of an innocent man. The lives of Barabbas and Jesus intersect in a way that seems random but stands as the perfect symbol of the central message of Calvary: "He made the one who did not know sin to be sin for us, so that in him we might become the righteousness of God" (2 Cor. 5:21).

✦ Who is Barabbas? ✦

Matthew calls him a "notorious" prisoner (Matt. 27:16). Mark adds more detail, informing readers that Barabbas was imprisoned with others who had committed murder during an uprising (Mark 15:7). John calls him someone who had "taken part in an uprising" (John 18:40 NIV). Peter, preaching at Pentecost, called Barabbas a "murderer" (Acts 3:14).

It's likely that Barabbas was all of these things. It's helpful for us to try to understand the mindset and the political tensions in first-century Rome to get a full understanding of this man who would cross paths with the Son of God at the apex of history. He didn't know he'd be swept up in salvation history, in the background of God's divine plan, fulfilled in the fullness of time. And yet here he is.

It's likely that Barabbas was part of a group of violently anti-Roman extremists. Many Jewish people in the first century were wary of Rome and strenuously resented the crushing oppression of the government. But the cohort of zealots to which Barabbas belonged to took resistance to another level. They sought to overthrow the Roman government by any means possible. And violence was often their calling card. This meant assassination plots, targeted murder, and terrorism. It's hard to compare then to now, the Roman system of government to our own, but perhaps the closest modern comparison might be a domestic terrorist group.

To understand the tumultuous times in which Barabbas was born, we need to go back a bit through the history of Israel in the time between the Old and New Testaments, often called by scholars as the "Second Temple Period." In exile in Babylon, some Jews were allowed to return to their home and rebuild their temple after the Persians defeated the Babylonians and King Cyrus II issued a decree in 538 BC. Israel became a Persian province until Alexander the Great conquered Persia; then the country fell into several hands, including Ptolemy of Egypt and then the Syrian Seleucid control. It was this last series of rulers who provoked the most resistance, especially a wicked governor named Antiochus Epiphanes, who banned Jewish rites and customs, including the Sabbath, circumcision, dietary laws, and temple sacrifices. He then built an altar to the false god Zeus. Such an attack on the religious life of the Jewish people sparked outrage and was the catalyst for what is often referred to as the Maccabean revolt. A priest named Mathias killed both a Syrian soldier and a Jewish priest preparing the sacrifice to Zeus. Mathias became an instant hero, and Israel assumed control of their religious practices and their country, cleansing the temple in a purification rite still celebrated by Jews every year as Hanukkah. Mathias's sons assumed leadership after his death. This family ruled Israel as an independent state until 63 BC, when Pompey, the Roman general, easily assumed control and Israel became a Roman province.

The Maccabees became legendary, almost messianic figures in Israel, and so every generation spawned some would-be freedom fighters. None were able to match the success of the first generation and overthrow their rulers. But that wasn't without trying. Rome, like Syria, often incited confrontations by desecrating the temple with Roman symbols, and exercised their power in often brutal and bloody ways.

However, Israel by this time was divided into various shades of engagement with Rome. Some were Jews who cast their lot with the Roman rulers—Herod and Pilate, for example. Others were skeptical but willing to work within the system. And then there were zealots like Barabbas who woke up every day plotting insurgency and rebellion. Men like Barabbas imagined themselves would-be Maccabees, heirs to the subversive agents who overthrew their overlord. And they resorted to any means necessary, often violence, including assassinations and random acts of terrorism such as stabbings of fellow Jews who were sympathetic to Rome.

The gospels describe Barabbas as "notorious" and Acts describes him as a murderer, so while some may have viewed him as a freedom fighter, most, even those who despised Rome, saw him as a bad man, a killer, worthy of punishment. Mark 15 and John 18 say that Barabbas took part in an uprising. And yet, this criminal would play a key role in the greatest drama in the history of the world.

✦ Jesus Barabbas and Jesus Christ ✦

In God's providence, in the mysterious outworking of His plan, two men, completely different in every single way, cross paths at the pivot point of history. Two men—Jesus Christ and Jesus Barabbas, as some early manuscripts referred to this notorious criminal.

We don't know if the two ever met, if when Jesus passed through Judea many times, Barabbas was within earshot or if Barabbas and his murderous thugs were in the crowd at the temple when Jesus spoke or turned over the tables of the money changers. It seems unlikely.

Barabbas, having unsuccessfully plotted an insurrection against Rome, languishing in a filthy prison with other convicted men, doubtless was not captivated by the message Jesus had. The one who would use any means necessary to live out his fantasy of being a freedom fighter would not take well to hearing Jesus urge love for enemies and of a kingdom not of this world. He'd love the critiques of the feckless religious authorities, often so subservient to their Roman overlords, protective of their power. But he probably recoiled when Jesus commended the faith of a centurion as being the greatest in Israel.

Their lives, so different. Jesus Christ, the child of a poor Nazareth couple, a rabbi who heals and restores, and Jesus Barabbas, a dangerous revolutionary, who tears down and destroys. One with unimpeachable character and perfect purity, and one whose guilt was known and established.

On the ground, circumstances put them together this way. Judas, once a devoted disciple, turns on his friend and delivers Jesus to the religious authorities who want Him dead. Jesus is first tried religiously by Annas, a former high priest who was no longer in power but still held wide influence over the rest of the religious community. Then He's brought before Caiaphas, the high priest, and then the full Sanhedrin.

All of them convicted Jesus of blasphemy. He claimed to be the Son of God, the Messiah, the promised one sent from God. They didn't believe Him, so this charge stuck. But they wanted Him dead, and only the Romans had the authority to do this, so it was off to Pontius Pilate, the governor of Judea.

Pilate's investigation found that Jesus was innocent of the charge the religious leaders were making, that He was attempting an insurrection against Rome. This charge was ironic on so many levels. First, languishing in a prison not far away was an actual insurrectionist, Barabbas. He'd easily plead guilty to this and die as a martyr for the cause of Jewish independence. Second, many of the Pharisees who made up the Sanhedrin sympathized with the desire to see Israel restored to self-rule, but they despised Jesus more for His claiming Messiahship, for His following among the people, for His incisive critiques of their hypocrisy.

Pilate first punted the decision to Herod, the governor of Galilee, Jesus' home region. But Herod passed on this hot potato and sent it back to Pilate. And so Pilate's second trick was to offer the Jewish people the release of one prisoner. This apparently was his custom every year, where Pilate, after Passover, would allow them the freeing of a prisoner as they celebrated their freedom from Egypt. Surely, Pilate speculated, they'd not side with their feckless leaders and they'd choose to let Jesus go. Jesus, whom they'd seen heal the sick and make the lame walk again. Jesus, who fed them in the wilderness and raised their dead.

And yet the leaders were able to stir up a bloodlust in the people.

The interactions between the crowds and Pilate are chilling to read, even two millennia later. Pilate laying out the facts of Jesus' innocence, and the mob, not caring about what is true, yelling, "Crucify Him! Crucify Him!"

They shouted with such fervor and passion. No love in their eyes, no ability to see Jesus' innocence. Instead they chose the contemptible Barabbas. No desire to weigh the facts carefully. Did they love Barabbas? I'm sure a segment of that crowd saw him as a freedom fighter, but most were probably moderate Jewish people who typically resisted the terrorist tactics of the zealots. Zealots like Barabbas had maybe killed friends and family members. Some historians have suggested that zealots would often hide among the crowds and knife people to death whom they thought too sympathetic to Rome.

So why was the crowd—the mob—so ready to vent their hatred? We don't know. Perhaps some, like Judas, were disappointed that Jesus refused to reign as an earthly king. Others perhaps were angered that Jesus claimed to be Messiah. And perhaps His message—personal repentance, self-denial, love, forgiveness, "blessed are the meek"—was one they didn't want to hear. The Jesus they wanted was not the Jesus who was and who is. Sadly, today this is true. Jesus is still very popular . . . unless we get too close.

The Jesus they wanted was not the Jesus who was and who is.

This is also a reminder of the way mobs often work. In the West we rightly celebrate democracy, where people have power instead of it being concentrated in a small group of people. Democracy has mostly served to lift people out of poverty and give voice to the marginalized. And yet there is a dark side to this when mobs are stirred to a frenzy and set their sights on punishing someone. Today we may seem to be more enlightened and progressive, but are we really? Witness the way mobs form online, sometimes egged on by influential figures and media outlets, toward a social scapegoat. And ask yourself how easy, how often, with a flick of the thumbs, it is to join in.

Just listen to this exchange with Pilate and the mobs:

At the festival Pilate used to release for the people a prisoner whom they requested. There was one named Barabbas, who was in prison with rebels who had committed murder during the rebellion. The crowd came up and began to ask Pilate to do for them as was his custom. Pilate answered them, "Do you want me to release the king of the Jews for you?" For he knew it was because of envy that the chief priests had handed him over. But the chief priests stirred up the crowd so that he would release Barabbas to them instead. Pilate asked them again, "Then what do you want me to do with the one you call the king of the Jews?"

> *Again they shouted, "Crucify him!"*
> *Pilate said to them, "Why? What has he done wrong?"*
> *But they shouted all the more, "Crucify him!"*
> *Wanting to satisfy the crowd, Pilate released Barabbas to them; and after having Jesus flogged, he handed him over to be crucified. (Mark 15:6–15)*

Pilate protesting Jesus' innocence, the crowds thirsting for vengeance, yelling "Crucify Him!" Some gospel writers have the crowds shouting this twice, an indication in the original Greek language of an unusually strong and impassioned plea. We judge, with the smugness

We'd be there in that crowd. We trade Barabbas for Jesus every day and don't flinch.

of someone who reads history and imagines ourselves the better, but we'd be there in that crowd, joining the unjust arrest of an innocent man. We trade Barabbas for Jesus every day and don't flinch.

There is such a mosaic of evil on display here at Jesus' trial: an unjust system of government, a violent terrorist with no regard for human life, a weak-willed leader, and perverted religion. In stark contrast, there stands the innocent One who is the antithesis of all of these. The fruits of sin's first seedling in the garden in full bloom: systemic injustice, murder, corruption, cruelty, converging on a lonely hill outside Jerusalem, where hung the Son of God. And so it is that at Easter we realize that the solution to the vexing sins that slither through God's good creation and so infest human hearts is that same crude instrument of torture, meant for Barabbas. At the cross we find the just One and the Justifier, the One who defeats the enemy powers and redeems the hearts of men.

✦ We Are All Barabbas Now ✦

Yet for Barabbas, he didn't know, couldn't have understood the role he'd play in human history. What was Barnabas thinking as he paced the cold, dank Roman cell in the tense hours before what he thought was the end of his life? He knew his crimes. He knew what lay ahead. Crucifixion by Rome was the cruelest form of capital punishment, reserved only for the most heinous of criminals and for slaves and foreigners. New Testament scholar Darrell Bock describes the process of crucifixion:

> Crucifixion had four steps. (1) The criminal had to carry the *patibulum* (the crossbeam) to the point of execution. The main stake was

already fixed in the ground at the execution site. (The cross was shaped like a capital T or, as in more traditional representations, a lowercase †.) (2) The condemned person would be bound to the crossbeam on the ground either by rope . . . or less frequently by nails. . . . (3) The beam would then be raised by forked poles and fastened to the upright pole (the length of which was so high that the condemned could get no support from his feet to breathe) or it was dropped into a slot at the top of the upright beam. (4) A tablet specifying the crime was hung around the accused to publicly declare the crime. Death came by suffocation through exhaustion or by loss of blood and body fluids. . . . Some estimate the cross's height at seven feet.[2]

This is the death that awaited Barabbas and the two fellow insurrectionists to be strung up alongside him. What went through Barabbas's mind, through the minds of the others, as they awaited the shuffle of the boots, the opening of the cell doors, and the rough hands of their executioners shoving them toward the ignominious hill outside Jerusalem? Was he recalling his life, regretting the path he chose for himself, one of a mercenary insurgent, a paid assassin for a hopeless cause? Was he thinking of his mother or father, his home, wherever that was? Was there any remorse? Repentance? Relief?

What he couldn't have known was that outside Pilate's court, there was a circus going on. He couldn't have known a furious and self-righteous multitude was setting its sights on another Jesus, Jesus of Nazareth. He had no idea that his life hung in the balance, between a weak governor and a raging mob, in the thin space between innocence and guilt.

The real story of Easter as seen through the eyes of Barabbas, the one that pulsates from this very scene and spills onto the pages of eternity, is not the injustice of a corrupt legal system or the dithering of Pontius Pilate or the dark turn of the people. The real story is that an innocent one, Jesus, died for the one who was so obviously and unapologetically guilty. If we cringe at this guilty man going free, we have to cringe at ourselves, who were just as guilty before God. The Bible tells us that every single member of the human race is Barabbas:

> *We all went astray like sheep;*
> *we all have turned to our own way;*
> *and the LORD has punished him*
> *for the iniquity of us all. (Isa. 53:6)*

> *There is no one righteous, not even one. (Rom. 3:10)*

This, of course, is not a popular sentiment, even at Easter. We don't dress up in our spring best and go to Grandma's house because we think we are depraved sinners, but the truth is that in the eyes of a holy God, everyone, from the saintliest saint to the most morally repugnant villain, is guilty. Convicted and sentenced, not by a powerless governor like Pilate or an unruly mob, but by God Himself.

And yet like Barabbas, we have the chance for freedom. Like Barabbas, we can shake off our chains, walk out of the prison of sin and death, and be given a miraculous and undeserving opportunity for new life.

I just love the way Sinclair Ferguson so eloquently writes about the juxtaposition of Barabbas and Jesus:

> Without knowing it, the religious leaders and Pilate and Barabbas were all part of a tapestry of grace which God was weaving for sinners. Their actions spoke louder than their words, louder than the cries of the crowds for Jesus' blood. Jesus was not dying for His own crimes,

but for the crimes of others; not for His own sins, but the sins of others. He did not die for Himself, He died for us![3]

Jesus was crucified for the crimes Barabbas committed. The One who resisted earthly revolution and urged respecting Caesar and paying taxes was crucified for treason while the one who plotted sedition was set free. The cross was meant for Barabbas. The cross was meant, really, for you and for me. Even a fellow insurrectionist could see this, whispering in his dying breaths:

> *"We are receiving the due reward of our deeds; but this man has done nothing wrong." And he said, "Jesus, remember me when you come into your kingdom." And he said to him, "Truly, I say to you, today you will be with me in paradise." (Luke 23:41–43 ESV)*

This promise, given by Jesus, is the real heart of Easter. The Son of God, the innocent One, pure and holy, God and man, went to that cross not ultimately because Pilate got it wrong or because the crowds lost their sense, but because this was God's divine rescue plan all along. The prophet Isaiah says of Jesus that "it pleased the LORD to bruise him" (Isa. 53:10 KJV). The entire sacrificial system in the Old Testament, the killing of innocent animals as an atonement for sin, all pointed to this moment when the Lamb of God would be slain for the sins of the world (1 John 2:2), crying in His final breaths, "It is finished." In many ways, that cross was made for Barabbas and it was made for sinners, like you and me, but it was really made for Jesus all along.

This was God's divine rescue plan all along.

Jesus died the death Barabbas should have died, paid the penalty for sin we should have paid but could not bear, and in exchange offers us freedom—freedom from sin and reconciliation with the Creator who made us. "For as in Adam all die, so also in Christ shall all be made alive" (1 Cor. 15:22 esv). This idea—that Christ is our substitute, that He took on the full wrath of God in our place—is central to the gospel, central to understanding what Easter is really all about.

In those lonely moments on the cross, as a bloody and bruised Jesus gasped for air, the entire burden of sin of God's people was thrust upon Him. This is why the earth grew dark, why the Father turned His face away. In that moment, the ugliness of sin—Barabbas's sins, our sins, the evil from the beginning to the end of time, was on Jesus' shoulders. He bore our sin. He took our shame. It is the greatest act of love in the world.

He made the one who did not know sin to be sin for us, so that in him we might become the righteousness of God. (2 Cor. 5:21)

Barabbas walked free, no charges against him. And so do you if you know Jesus as Savior and Lord. "There is therefore no condemnation for those who are in Christ Jesus" (Rom. 8:1 esv). You bear no guilt. You carry no shame. You are reconciled with your Creator.

I have always wondered what happened to Barabbas. What did he do with his new chance at life? Did he go back to his devilish ways, or did he look up at the cross where he should have been and wonder, in awe, how God spared his life? I want to imagine, though there is no tradition or proof that this actually happened, that Barabbas is there among many disciples gathered in Galilee, when a resurrected Jesus declares that God has given Him all authority in heaven and earth. When Jesus urges people to declare the gospel to the nations. I want to think that Barabbas not only saw Jesus as the unlucky innocent who was killed to satiate the bloodlust of a crowd, but the spotless Lamb of God who took his place, that he saw Jesus as both his physical and eternal substitute for sin. We don't know. Maybe we will see him in heaven. Maybe we'll call him brother Barabbas.

What we do know—what you can know this Easter—is that the innocent one nailed to the cross was nailed there for you. He bore your sins and took your punishment so you could have abundant and eternal life. Will you look up at that cross this Easter season and see your Savior?

STUDY QUESTIONS:

- Consider the life of a revolutionary like Barabbas and the ends-justifies-the-means mentality.

    - Compare and contrast Barabbas's idea of revolution with Jesus' revolution of love.
    - Compare and contrast the charges against Barabbas and the charges against Jesus.

- Consider why the crowds and the religious leaders chose to save the life of Barabbas in exchange for Jesus' life.

- Meditate on Jesus as a substitute for the convicted criminal Barabbas and Jesus as a substitute for your sin.

SUGGESTED HYMNS AND SONGS:

Hallelujah, What a Savior!—Phillip Bliss
In My Place—Michael Bleeker

CHAPTER FIVE

The Powerless

Pilate

. . . I believe . . . in Jesus Christ, his only Son, our Lord,
who was conceived by the Holy Spirit
and born of the virgin Mary.
He suffered under Pontius Pilate,
was crucified, died, and was buried . . .

THE APOSTLES' CREED

"You would have no authority over me at all," Jesus answered him,
"if it hadn't been given you from above. This is why the one who
handed me over to you has the greater sin."

JOHN 19:11

S uffered under Pontius Pilate" declares the oldest Christian creed, recited, memorized, and internalized by millions of Christians throughout the history of the church. But why single out Pilate? Why doesn't the great creed mention Judas the betrayer, or the conspiring Pharisees and scribes, or the disciples who ran in fear?

No, they were left out. Instead, the Apostles' Creed mentions a mid-level Roman politician who would have been but a mere footnote in the history of the Roman Empire, forgotten by history and otherwise unremarkable. Why is Pontius Pilate in the ancient affirmation of faith, juxtaposed so ignominiously against the seemingly powerless figure whom he tried so hard to avoid?

Most historians and scholars believe the church fathers, so eager to put to words the core tenets of what they read of the Apostles in their copies of the Scriptures, included Pilate because they wanted to establish a historical marker for succeeding generations. Pontius Pilate was an actual figure with a tenure as governor of Judea during the time Jesus lived. The history could be researched and located and confirmed. And today this fact continues to bolster the case for the truth of the Christian story. And we have archeological evidence for Pilate's rule. In 1961, a block of limestone was discovered in Caesarea Philippi that bore a dedication by a "Pilate, prefect of Judea."

But there's a much more subtle reason the early church insisted on the name of Pontius Pilate in the ancient creed. It's a reminder of a showdown between two rival sources of power: the kingdom of men, stewarded by shallow but powerful men like Pilate, and the kingdom of God which arrived in humility in a lonely rabbi from Nazareth, unjustly arrested and brutally tortured, bearing a mock robe and crown of thorns. It's as if this line in the creed exists to remind us of the conflict of the ages, between the seed of the woman and the seed of the serpent, predicted by God in the Garden of Eden and reaching its climax in a dusty backwater Roman province right before the Jewish Passover.

✦ Who Is Pilate? ✦

When I think of Pontius Pilate, my mind always goes to the classic film *Ben-Hur* and the character played to perfection by Australian actor Frank Thring. I see an average, middle-aged man with a close-cropped haircut and a dad bod. Usually, for whatever reason, Pilate has a wispy goatee and sandals. In Easter pageants, it seems any guy can play Pilate. The casting call is usually the deacon's bench. All you need is a robe, a bald spot, and a look of bewilderment.

But Pontius Pilate was a real person in place and time, more than the cardboard cutout we envision in movies and plays and flannel-graphs. So who is this ruler who suddenly shows up to coldly wash his hands in defiance of a mob determined to crucify Jesus? We don't really know much about where he was born or his family, though some have speculated that perhaps he was born in Italy.

To fully understand Pontius Pilate, it's helpful to zoom out a bit and understand some of the history that placed this rising Roman politician on a collision course with an itinerant rabbi from Nazareth. It begins with Herod. And not just one Herod, but a succession of Herods appointed by the Romans to rule this part of the world. Yes, there are several Herods who ruled that part of the world, and it can get confusing trying to sort them all out.

The first was Herod the Great, who ruled the entire region for forty years, right up until the time of Jesus' birth. This Herod was a legendary builder who created some of the amazing architectural masterpieces in the world, including large aqueducts that brought water from the Mediterranean around Israel, and the Jewish temple, a marvel that elicited awe and wonder every time a pilgrim came to worship (Mark 13:1). Today those aqueducts are still mostly standing. I've visited them on tours of Israel. Herod's temple, though destroyed by the Roman general Titus in AD 70, still has its Western Wall visible and is a revered symbol of Judaism, visited by pilgrims from around the world.

But Herod was not loved. He was feared. Deep insecurities shaped the way he led, including his paranoia about being replaced. He had three sons and a wife killed. He committed infanticide against baby boys in Bethlehem (Matt. 2) upon hearing the news from the Magi that Jesus, a new King of the Jews, would be born. Herod was so ruthless and cruel that Caesar Augustus once said that it would be better to have been Herod's pig than his son.[1] It's not a compliment when a Caesar thinks you are a bit too authoritarian.

When Herod the Great died, his will dictated that the vast territory he ruled be divided among this three remaining sons, Herod Phillip, Herod Antipas, and Herod Archelaus. Herod Antipas, whose territory included Galilee, is the ruler who ordered John the Baptist beheaded for speaking out about Antipas' adultery with Herod Phillip's wife. Antipas is also the ruler before whom Jesus would appear in His trial.

Herod Archelaus was the lesser of the three sons and seemed to inherit his father's cruelty. He was also inept. In fact, he was so bad that a delegation of Jewish leaders traveled to Rome and successfully petitioned Caesar to replace him. For Rome, Judea was strategic, an important bridge between Egypt and Syria. They couldn't afford tumult in the region, so they quickly cycled through a series of governors to replace Herod, none of whom seemed to be able to solidify control.

Eventually they landed on Pontius Pilate, a mid-level Roman politician. Pilate was recommended by a benefactor high up in the Roman government named Sejanus.[2] Judea was not exactly a plum posting for an aspiring politician. It was a complex situation with a history of messy revolts and unrest. Rulers got into trouble when they failed to recognize the importance and significance of the sacred rituals and practices of the Jewish people. So Rome came to a kind of arrangement that gave Israel some religious autonomy, deferring to its seventy-member religious ruling council, called the Sanhedrin, and a security force of temple guards. Jews were given space to practice their sacrifices and rituals. But if this wasn't managed well, things could spiral out of control quickly. Perhaps Pilate accepted the assignment thinking it could be a stepping-stone to something greater. But even though he was likely the most successful at governing Judea, he too got caught in the leadership quicksand. He developed a reputation for brutality. Historians tell us about a few notable flashpoints:

- ✦ Not long after he assumed power in Judea, he ordered Roman soldiers to place large defensive shields bearing the likeness of Caesar in Jerusalem. This was a cultural and racial affront to the Jewish people, a highly insensitive gesture that Pilate did to try to ingratiate himself to Tiberius, but which brought tremendous opposition from the Jewish people. Jewish people protested and even followed him to his palace in Caesarea. He eventually backed down.[3]

- ✦ To fund a freshwater source in Jerusalem, Pilate raided the temple treasury for funds, again provoking backlash. This time Pilate put down the protest by hiding Roman soldiers in the crowd, disguised as protesters. His soldiers used knives to kill many Jewish people.[4]

✦ His Roman troops massacred some Galileans while they were worshiping in the temple, their blood mixing with the blood of the sacrifices (Luke 13:1).

Pilate could be brutal and cruel, but it cost him. By the time Jesus was put on trial before him, Pilate had zero political capital and his standing with Rome was on thin ice. Not only had he squandered his leadership capital, but Sejanus, the benefactor who had recommended Pilate for this posting to the emperor, Tiberius, was off the scene, caught up in a scandal of his own, and executed. Every move of the prefect's was being watched. He couldn't afford another uprising. He couldn't afford his troubles to reach the ears of Rome.

✦ An Agonizing Choice ✦

So when we open the gospels and read about Pontius Pilate, it's good to remember that there is a history that informs and influences the decisions he makes. He's a man hanging onto his position, who despises the people he is tasked with leading. He has a tenuous alliance with the religious leaders, but you can hear the desperation in his voice and see the uneasiness with which he handles the trial of Jesus. He both disdains these people and is scared of what will happen with his position.

Jesus' trial was in three parts. There was the religious inquisition, first by Annas and Caiaphas, then the full Sanhedrin, and finally the legal proceedings in front of Pilate. The religious trial was for blasphemy and happened in front of both Annas, the retired high priest who was a sort of godfather figure among the Sanhedrin, and Caiaphas, the actual chief priest, appointed by Pilate but beholden to Annas. Jesus was also given a hearing before the full Sanhedrin, the Jewish ruling council.

The religious leaders needed the Roman government in this case because they didn't just want to reprimand Jesus. They wanted Him dead. Blasphemy, according to Jewish law, should result in stoning. But while Rome sometimes looked the other way when the chief priests sought to put people to death (John 10:31; Acts 7:58), only Rome had the authority to carry the kind of state execution they wanted to see Jesus suffer.

But why did they hate Him so much?

There are many reasons for the religious leaders' animus toward Jesus. One was His claims of deity, though His works fulfilled the Scriptures' definition of a Messiah. But it's more likely that they saw Jesus as a threat to their way of life. This arrangement with Rome gave them power. And Jesus directly criticized and exposed the religious leaders' hypocrisy. So it seems they wanted a state execution as a kind of national rejection of Jesus. Perhaps they thought the execution and shameful death of their leader would quash the Jesus movement. After all, the law held that a person who was put to death by hanging was "cursed" (Deut. 21:22–23). In their thinking, no true Messiah would submit Himself to such an ignominious death.

And yet this very method of death would become an apologetic for Jesus' divinity. One of the most observant Jews of this period, who studied under the best teachers, would later convert to the Jesus movement and write, "Christ redeemed us from the curse of the law by becoming a curse for us—for it is written, "Cursed is everyone who is hanged on a tree" (Gal. 3:3 ESV).

In order to see their nemesis put to death in the most cruel and shaming way, they dragged Jesus to Pilate's Jerusalem palace, the Praetorium near the temple. They couldn't enter, so they negotiated with Pilate outside his palace, petitioning the governor to execute Jesus by crucifixion. Their charge recorded by Luke: subversion. He was a threat to the Roman state, they said:

> *"We found this man misleading our nation, opposing payment of taxes to Caesar, and saying that he himself is the Messiah, a king."* (Luke 23:2)

These are serious charges. First, a charge of insurrection: misleading the nation, stirring up revolution. This is the very crime Barabbas and the two thieves were arrested for. In a sense, they are saying to Pilate, "We know how serious you are about peace and about capturing anyone who desires to subvert Rome's rule. Here is another domestic terrorist, another threat to our peace."

Second, they lied and said that Jesus opposed paying taxes to Caesar. Jesus had specifically urged Jewish people to "render to Caesar the things that are Caesar's" (Mark 12:17 esv). Yes, these religious leaders who were tasked with shepherding God's people twisted Jesus' words in order to see Him arrested for sedition.

Lastly, they used a novel interpretation of Jesus' messianic claims to make the charge that Jesus was trying to overthrow the Roman rule and lead an attempted coup. Jesus did claim, often, that the kingdom of God was near and that He was the rightful king. But He also predicted His own death and betrayal. He resisted those who wanted to make Him an earthly king (John 6:15).

What's ironic is that the very things the Sanhedrin charged Jesus with, the articles of indictment they handed to Pilate, were beliefs many Jewish people held. Most despised the exorbitant taxes the Romans collected. Most longed for a day when a new and successful overthrow of Roman power would usher in God's kingdom. But so incensed were they by Jesus' revelation of their hypocrisy and sin, so angered at Jesus' claims of deity, the religious leaders suddenly became loyal Romans, defending the honor of an Emperor they despised ("We have no king but Caesar!"). Dark hearts often make unlikely allies.

And now this political hand grenade lands in Pilate's lap. What does he do? Clearly the Sanhedrin is not operating in good faith. Let's remember, they technically conducted an unjust trial, with false testimony. They'd already violated Jesus' civil rights by abusing Him at the trial. And they were calling for an innocent man to be executed by the state. They were way above the ceremonial law here. But they assumed by shoving it over to Pilate and asking for him to sign off on the crucifixion, their hands would be clean.

Imagine Pilate's nightmare. He is already weakened by his previous missteps and his clumsy efforts to correct them. He is on thin ice in Rome. And he can't even find solace at home, where his wife, who some historians believed may have become a closet follower of Jesus, pleads with Pilate to release Jesus after being disturbed by a dream the night before the trial (Matt. 27:19).

One more incident of unrest and Rome could come calling. And when rulers in the Empire were recalled, they weren't simply reassigned, they were often executed or forced to commit suicide. This is why they insisted to Pilate: "If you release this man, you are not Caesar's friend"(John 19:12). Pilate faced an agonizing choice with few good options. This was the biggest crisis of his political life.

Pilate had no desire to get pulled into the internal machinations of a religion he didn't even understand or respect. This is why he tried so hard to defer the case back to them. This is why he asks Jesus, "Are you the king of the Jews?" (Luke 23:3). In other words, he is pleading with Jesus, *Can you not just work this out with your people?* When he declared the first time, "I find no grounds for charging this man" (Luke 23:4), he's saying, "There is no crime against Rome here." Thinking like a prosecutor, Pilate is telling the religious leaders they don't have a legal case against Jesus. But the religious leaders would not yield.

In a series of back-and-forth negotiations held outside Pilate's palace (because to enter his courts before Passover would violate the law), the Sanhedrin insisted Jesus be executed by the state. So they brought up Jesus on charges against the Roman Empire. They accused Jesus of stirring up the people (Luke 23:5). What was he to do? Pilate had to figure out a way to solve this riddle of Jesus. He had two chess moves. First, he tried to defer the trial to Herod, who was in town for the Passover and Festival of Unleavened Bread. The members of the Sanhedrin mentioned Jesus had begun stirring up people with his teaching "in Galilee." Galilee was Herod's jurisdiction.

Would this work? Herod's standing with Rome was better. If he rendered a judgment, it could give Pilate cover. But Herod also was a canny politician. Luke 23:8 says that he actually looked forward to meeting Jesus. He'd heard of His exploits and was hoping Jesus would perform some miracles in front of him, but of course Jesus wasn't a court jester or a magician on demand. So the silent Son of God was sent back to Pilate. If Herod couldn't be entertained by Jesus, he would spend no political capital engaging Him.

So Pilate is back to square one. He has one more move. Every year at this time of year, it was his custom to release a Jewish prisoner close to the day Jewish people commemorated Passover. This was an attempt to build goodwill at the time when Jewish people celebrated their own freedom from bondage in Egypt. Perhaps the mere arrest and embarrassment of Jesus, dressed up in a mock robe and an ugly crown of thorns on His head, would be enough humiliation to satisfy the anger of the religious authorities and put down the movement. But the death angel that passed over the houses of Jewish people in Egypt would not pass over the Son of God that day. The Sanhedrin's bloodlust would not be satiated.

Instead, they cried out for the release of a dangerous criminal, a domestic terrorist who led an insurrection against Rome. Barabbas was no friend of the Sanhedrin, who were appointed by Pilate and sympathetic to Rome. They considered Barabbas's exploits an embarrassment at best and a threat to their base of power at worst.

The Sanhedrin gathered allies, a mob who insisted on Jesus being crucified. Out of options, the governor finally had Jesus flogged, a torturous punishment that leaves a victim barely able to walk. Perhaps this literal pound of flesh would be enough to satiate the Sanhedrin, but no. They wanted their problem, Jesus, silenced. For Pilate, his future was flashing before his eyes. He *knew* Jesus was innocent, unworthy of Roman execution. And yet he also knew that if he released Jesus, a riot would ensue and he'd probably be recalled to Rome, a failure. So he washed his hands and turned the Innocent One over to be crucified.

> The death angel that passed over the houses of Jewish people in Egypt would not pass over the Son of God that day.

♦ Are You a King? ♦

There are so many mysteries and paradoxes in Pilate's role in the Easter story. Here is a man who despised the people he governed, who used brute force to crush dissent and yet is in such a weak position that he essentially has to capitulate to the demands of the mob. Pilate holds an office. He is sitting in a palace. He makes pronouncements. But he's powerless.

It is interesting to me the conflict that is happening in Pilate's conscience this whole time. Not a man given to mercy, he nevertheless seems compelled to defend Jesus' innocence. Why is it that Pilate fought so hard for a wandering rabbi he hardly knew? Did he see something different in Jesus?

What we do know is that Pilate, like many throughout the ages, desperately tried to avoid the central question of Jesus. And Jesus didn't let Pilate escape. He wouldn't give Pilate what he needed to secure His own release and save Pilate a headache. On one level, Pilate is a tragic figure swept into the pages of human history, thrust into a collision with the Son of God.

We have to look beyond the surface and see the cosmic battle taking place at Jesus' trial. It is not only Jesus being put on trial here. It is Pilate being put on trial before Jesus. D. A. Carson says, "There is an implicit invitation in Jesus' words. The man in the dock invites his judge to be his follower, to align himself with those who are 'of the truth.' Jesus is not dangerous; he may also be getting under Pilate's skin."[5]

Getting under Pilate's skin was Jesus' true purpose in this moment. Jesus' destiny was already set. He was going to the cross. He accepted the cup of God's wrath in the garden. He stood down the armies of heaven. He fulfilled the long-held prophecies of a suffering servant, the one whom God was "pleased to crush" for the sins of His people (Isa. 53:10). And in being charged by the religious leaders and executed by the Romans, Jesus would be put on the cross by both Jew and Gentile and by every sinner whose burden Jesus bore. The mendacity of the religious leaders and the weakness of Pilate were mere instruments in the hands of God.

Back in the chambers, away from the crowd and from the religious leaders, the one who seems to hold all the power in the world, Pilate, is confronted in his own soul by the One who comes in weakness and yet upholds the universe by His hands. It is not the one in the stately robes, the one whose mere words could send people to their deaths, who is really in charge. It's the One who comes in bloodied from Roman whips, mocked with uncountable indignities, abandoned even by His own disciples. That's the paradox of the Passion.

John's gospel contains the richest dialogue between Jesus and Pilate. Pilate was getting a theology lesson in those private chambers. First, Jesus teaches Pilate about His kingship. Everyone—from the religious leaders, to Pilate, to the crowds—knew that Jesus wasn't fomenting the kind of insurrection that Barabbas was plotting, but the kingdom Jesus spoke of was threatening in a different way. "Are you the king of the Jews?" (John 18:33). Pilate asked the Galilean. Jesus said that His kingdom is "not of this world" (John 18:36).

> Pilate thought he was trying to save Jesus, but Jesus was really trying to save Pilate.

We often mistake Jesus' words to mean that the kingdom is something ethereal, above the world. But Jesus is saying that the kingdom of God is above the temporary battles and skirmishes that we often waste energy fighting over. The kingdom of God is bigger than Pilate and the Sanhedrin, both of which would lose power within a generation. The kingdom of God is God's righteous rule in Christ, over the whole expanse of the world. It's the redemption of human hearts, and the renewal of the cosmos. It's bringing heaven to earth. God's kingdom was not of the world Pilate was immediately looking at, which is why Jesus didn't marshal angel armies, why He stopped His followers from brandishing swords. His pathway to the throne went through the very cross Pilate was trying to spare Him.

Pilate thought he was trying to save Jesus, but Jesus was really trying to save Pilate. Jesus' life seemed to hang in the balance, but He was in full control of His future. Rather, it was Pilate's soul hanging in the balance.

"You are a king then?" Pilate asks, bewildered. To which Jesus says, "I was born for this, and I have come into the world for this: to testify to the truth. Everyone who is of the truth listens to my voice" (John 18:37). Romans were superstitious, often appropriating the gods of the nations they conquered, and holding their Caesars up as gods. But you can hear the searching in Pilate's queries. *Where are you from, Jesus?* His mind is searching. Perhaps he wondered if Jesus was "half divine," the son of one of the gods whom Romans believed often inhabited the souls of men.[6] Pilate is clearly trying to save himself, but he's also confused, perhaps intrigued by the man who sits in front of him, fearless and quiet Jesus, so different from the religious leaders who sought to kill Him.

In His answer, Jesus is telling Pilate that there is one, not multiple, sources of truth, and it centered not on a set of principles but a Person. Pilate couldn't understand that the answer to his whole life, his very meaning and existence was in front of him, in the person of Jesus

Christ. This was no coincidence. This was no mere political dilemma. This was a divine appointment with his Creator.

> *So Pilate said to him, "Do you refuse to speak to me? Don't you*
> *know that I have the authority to release you and the authority*
> *to crucify you?"*
>   *"You would have no authority over me at all," Jesus answered*
> *him, "if it hadn't been given you from above. This is why the one*
> *who handed me over to you has the greater sin." (John 19:10–11)*

What a stunning answer. The one who stood seemingly helpless before Roman is the One who actually has all the power. Jesus, we are told by the writer of Hebrews, "upholds the universe by the word of his power" (Heb. 1:3 ESV). In every generation, kings raise themselves up as would-be gods, but they are no match for the quiet, eternal power of the real King. So though Jesus "suffered under Pontius Pilate," it would be Pilate who would ultimately suffer if he did not humble himself before the real power: the one whom God has given a name above all names and has crowned with glory and honor.

> To ask "What is truth?" is to make an assertion that nothing can be knowable.

And yet Jesus is aiming straight for Pilate's heart. As if to say, *You don't quite want to be here, in this position with your entire political future on the line. You don't understand what is happening. And I am here to help you see into your soul and find salvation.*

Pilate's response, "What is truth?" is a common intellectual dodge made by people who don't seem to actually want truth. It's the sad song of every age, as people try to escape the inescapable and avoid the question of Jesus. To ask "What is truth?" is different than the honest quest for truth we see in Thomas's doubts. To ask, "What is truth?" is to make an assertion that nothing can be knowable, that truth is subjective, unfixed, informed by experience. Without a confrontation with the truth, without bowing to the Author of truth, our hearts will be subject to the whims of every age and, like Pilate, will yield our consciences to what is most convenient.

Jesus knew that this moral relativism is in and of itself a declaration of truth, but an empty one. Deep in Pilate's heart and in every heart is a longing to understand the meaning of life, to know and be known by the One who declares Himself the way, the truth, and the life (John 14:6).

In the end, despite Jesus' "I am here to help you" invitation, Pilate caved in to the demands of the religious leaders and wrote a death sentence for an innocent man. Yet I'm struck by the way Pilate presented Jesus for death. After the beating, Pilate stood Jesus before the hostile crowd and declared, "Behold the man!" (John 19:5 ESV). More than anything this is Pilate giving the people what they desire—okay, here is your scapegoat, your pound of flesh. But he is also unknowingly making a theological declaration. Jesus is "the man," the fullest expression of the *Imago Dei,* the second Adam from above, come to restore what the first Adam destroyed. And Pilate made another statement, intended for mockery but proclaiming an eternal truth: He ordered a sign nailed to Jesus' cross: "Jesus of Nazareth, the King of the Jews" (John 19:19). Jesus is the king of the Jews, promised through the ages, declared by the prophets, the One whom God told David would sit on his throne forever (2 Sam. 7:16). God used Pilate's condescending language to declare the gospel across the ages.

How did this experience change Pilate? We don't really know. The last time we see Pilate in the Gospels is at his release of Jesus' body to some secret Jesus followers for a proper burial. And we see him deploying a troop of Roman soldiers to guard the tomb, at the request of the religious leaders.

We have to imagine this didn't register for Pilate as just another day at the office. He had presided over countless crucifixions of insurrectionists and murderers—but none who spoke with the clarity and power of this Jesus of Nazareth. None whose death caused an earthquake and the sudden descent of night. None whose followers claimed that He had risen from the dead three days later. Did Jesus' invitation to Pilate echo in the man's heart and mind as he went home, as he slept, as he discussed Jesus with his wife, who was still haunted by her dream about His innocence?

Historians tell us Pilate eventually did lose his governorship as a result of one last bad political move, putting down another uprising, this time by Samaritans. Some believe he was recalled to Rome and forced to commit suicide, a common fate for failed leaders.[7] Paul Maier's novel, *Pontius Pilate*, imagines a late-in-life conversion, just before he dies, the result of years of praying and prodding by his wife, a convert to Christianity.

What we do know is that the questions Jesus asked of Pilate on the first Easter, He asks of every human soul. And the words of life Jesus both offered and made available by His death and resurrection are still available to those who look up to that ugly Roman cross and find their Savior. Alistair Begg says it this way:

> Each of us have to come to the point where we determine "Who is Jesus?" "Why did He come, what did He do, and does it even matter?" It will not be enough for us to try and fudge the decision off as Pilate

did. There are no bowls available in the auditorium at the moment for the washing of our hands of the responsibility. There is no place for us to hide. There is no place that we can ultimately hide from God. Jesus stands in the Hall of Pilate, waiting for Pilate to make a decision. One day Pilate will stand in the Hall of Jesus, and Jesus will pronounce the verdict.[8]

This Easter, as you contemplate the tragic and mysterious life of Pilate, ask yourself these questions: *Will you humble yourself before the King of kings? Will you look up at this bloodied Galilean and see your Savior? Will you look in on this empty tomb and understand that God is renewing and restoring all things?*

STUDY QUESTIONS:

◆ Consider the quandary of Pontius Pilate. He didn't want to deal with the "Jesus" question, but was forced by history and by the sovereign plan of God to come face-to-face with the Son of God. Why is the question of Jesus so unavoidable?

◆ Pilate had several opportunities to wrestle with the claims of Jesus. Explain all of these moments and what they mean.

◆ Read through John's description of the interaction between Pilate and Jesus. Who was really on trial? What was Jesus trying to do?

◆ Pilate was in the seat of power and yet before Jesus he seemed powerless. What does this tell us about the power of governments and the power of God?

SUGGESTED HYMNS AND SONGS:

In Christ Alone—Keith and Kristyn Getty
Crown Him with Many Crowns—Matthew Bridges

The Doubter

Thomas

Incarnate Deity is a thought that was never invented by poet's mind, nor reasoned out by philosopher's skill. Incarnate Deity, the notion of the God that lived, and bled, and died in human form, instead of guilty man, it is itself its own best witness. The wounds are the infallible witness of the gospel of Christ.[1]

CHARLES SPURGEON

Thomas responded to him, "My Lord and my God!"

JOHN 20:28

He was an award-winning journalist for the *Chicago Tribune* when a near fatal incident with one of his children caused his wife to explore the claims of Christianity. Lee, an atheist, was sure his wife had gone off the deep end. So Lee applied his journalistic mind to the claims of Christianity, determined to prove his wife wrong and dismiss the validity of her newfound faith. However, in the course of his investigation, something happened. The evidence for Jesus' resurrection became too voluminous to overcome, too hard to dismiss. And Lee Strobel became a Christian, his testimony told in the bestselling book *The Case for Christ*, which has since helped thousands of former skeptics find their own way to Jesus.

Church history is filled with people like Lee Strobel, doubters and skeptics who are compelled by the evidence and are drawn in by the Spirit of God toward faith. And in this chapter, I'd like to look at the compelling testimony of Christianity's first skeptic, Thomas, who turned from disciple to doubter to devoted. Thomas's place in the Easter story is a beacon of hope to hurt, wandering, displaced souls who long to find their way home.

✦ I Will Die with You ✦

Unlike some of the other disciples, we don't really have the exact details of Thomas's early life and his calling. The three synoptic gospels (Matthew, Mark, and Luke) only record Thomas as being included in the list of the twelve men Jesus called to leave their lives behind and follow Him. The only detail we know from Thomas is that he was a twin (John 11:16). It's likely that, like the other disciples except for Judas, he was from the Galilee region.

But while we don't hear much from Thomas in most of the gospels, we can see him there as Jesus commissions the Twelve and sends them out to preach the good news of the kingdom. We can observe him in the ship, watching Jesus walk on the water. We can envision his stunned silence when Jesus calms a raging sea or makes the lame walk or raises dead people from the grave. His hands were full of food when Jesus took a little boy's lunch that day on the hillside and fed His people in the wilderness.

We do know that Thomas left everything to follow this itinerant rabbi. Something in Jesus compelled this young man to abandon his livelihood and risk his entire life on Jesus. When others left or faded away, Thomas was one of the few who stayed. When Judas slipped out of the Upper Room, Thomas was still there, hearing Jesus' haunting and prophetic words about His arrest, death, and resurrection. He listened, likely with bewilderment, as Jesus taught about a new future he was creating, a Spirit-fueled movement that would be built on the foundation of these eleven ordinary men. Thomas quailed when Jesus prophesied Judas' betrayal, wondering, like the others, if he had the

> While "doubting" has become the favorite adjective for Thomas, we must first know him as a brave follower of Jesus who risked it all.

seed of disloyalty in his own heart. He heard the footsteps of the soldiers as they came for Jesus. He saw the images of a bloody Jesus. He experienced the loss and separation of the One who had called him friend.

This is what Thomas saw. So while "doubting" has become the favorite adjective for Thomas, we must first know him as a brave follower of Jesus who risked it all.

Only the gospel of John gives us any words from Thomas and though they are few, they are profound and give us insight into his character. In John 11, Jesus and the Twelve were in a small town on the other side of the Jordan from Judea, near the place where John the Baptist began his ministry of baptism. Word got back to them that one of Jesus' dearest friends, Lazarus, brother of Mary and Martha, was dying. Lazarus was in Bethany, four days' journey away, so it was imperative for Jesus to go back and see His friend. Strangely, Jesus didn't rush back but instead lingered for two more days. He reassured the disciples that Lazarus was not merely dead, but sleeping. At the time they of course didn't know what was coming. His desire in waiting was for Lazarus to be so dead, four days dead, that nobody could doubt the miracle of his resurrection. Jesus' purpose in returning to Bethany was not just to raise His friend but to raise faith in those who witnessed the miracle, including the disciples.

But there were also other worries about going back toward Judea. The anger of Jesus' enemies among the religious leaders was rising and word was going around about plots to take Jesus and possibly kill Him. Jesus' growing movement and His claims to be the Son of God, the Savior of the world, so incensed them that they had tried to seize Him (John 10:38–39). They had just slipped away across the Jordan to this hideaway where they'd be safe. So the disciples were understandably nervous. They weighed the risks, discussing a trip back into the hot zone. Of course they loved their friend Lazarus, but if he was already dead, was it worth going back and risking Jesus' death and their own? You can hear them carefully weighing the pros and cons, oblivious, it would seem, that they were traveling with the Author of Life, who breathed life into Adam and would breathe life back into Lazarus and one day walk out of a tomb, defeating the death that stole the breath from His friend. Jesus would submit to death on the cross, but it would happen on the Father's timeline, not at the whims of His enemies.

Jesus, of course, was determined to go, to show the world a glimpse of His resurrection power, a porthole into the new creation. And so Thomas, after hearing and perhaps participating in this heated deliberation, was the first one to volunteer to go with Jesus. "Let's go too so that we may die with him" (John 11:16).

It's kind of a macabre response, perhaps giving us insight into Thomas's more pessimistic personality. It seems Thomas was the one always counting the cost, weighing the facts, looking for certainty when others like Peter were guided by the more emotional and subjective compass of the heart. And Thomas didn't understand all that he even said. Thomas or any of the other disciples couldn't really go with Jesus to die. To pay for the sins of the world, Jesus had to go alone to the garden, alone to the cross, alone to the grave.

And yet in a sense, Thomas understood the call Jesus gives every disciple to come and die with Him. Because He went alone, we too can take up our cross and we can die with Him. Paul would later say that he was "crucified with Christ" and no longer lives so that the life of Christ can be lived through him (Gal. 2:20).

This is a bold statement. Thomas seems like the silent one, who carefully weighs and thinks before coming to a conclusion, and yet when he speaks, it is a profound statement of courage and loyalty. "Let's go die with Jesus" could be a life verse, the call of everyone who sees and believes Jesus.

Which is why if we only think of Thomas as "doubting," we miss out on who Thomas is altogether. Before he was "Doubting Thomas," he was "Brave Thomas," willing to put it all on the line for the one he loved. This will help us, I think, process his struggles after the crucifixion.

✦ "How Can We Know the Way?" ✦

The second time we hear Thomas speak—again, with the same thoughtful, careful precision and inquiry—is during Jesus' discourse in the Upper Room on the night in which He would be betrayed, arrested, and marched to the cross. They were sharing a Passover meal, leaning in close to hear the Master share His last words. Jesus had dismissed Judas and was sharing about both His pending death and resurrection and His plan to leave the disciples and send the Spirit of God. A new movement was afoot and these eleven men would be the foundation of the church.

It was overwhelming news. Thomas and the others had given up all they had to walk with Jesus for three years. They'd grown close to Him. He was their rabbi, their teacher, their Master, but most importantly, their friend. He'd washed their feet. He'd shared countless meals with them. They'd laughed and argued and cried together. They had listened to Him weave stories about what the kingdom of God is like, stories about how the lost can be found. Jesus had empowered them to do things beyond their capacity and human ability: to cast out demons, to heal the sick, and to preach and teach about the coming kingdom of God.

Now Jesus was telling them that this was coming to an end. Jesus' enemies, the religious leaders who refused to see and acknowledge His divinity, were closing in. And Jesus wouldn't summon the forces of heaven to defend Himself. Instead, He'd submit to the Father's will—and die. And just as the world hated Jesus, they'd also hate the disciples and everyone who would dare call Jesus Lord.

Yet Jesus offered words of comfort and assurance. "Don't let your heart be troubled. Believe in God; believe also in me" (John 14:1). They did believe in God. And they did believe in Jesus. Peter had spoken for the others when he declared that Jesus was *the* Christ, the Son of the living God (Matt. 16:16–18), and when he expressed their utter dependence on Jesus: "To whom will we go?" (John 6:68).

But what did believing in Jesus mean? They, unlike us, didn't have the full written canon of God's Word. They couldn't thumb through the gospels and didn't yet have an Easter to celebrate. "If I go away and prepare a place for you," Jesus said, "I will come again and take you to myself, so that where I am you may be also. You know the way to where I am going" (John 14:3–4).

Thomas, the seeker, the inquirer, the analyzer, asked, "Lord, we don't know where you're going. How can we know the way?" (John 14:5). This is a good question. Thomas, you remember, was the one willing to "go and die" with Jesus. Thomas is willing to obey Jesus at all costs, but he just needs to know where to go.

Jesus is going to prepare a place for them and for us, and He had to go alone. The place He's preparing is both a future in the kingdom of heaven but also a place of rest in peace with the Father. This is why only Jesus could go. Only Jesus could separate the wall that divides sinful humans from their Creator. Thomas couldn't go and atone for his own sins. And neither can we. Jesus went alone to the cross so we could go with Him.

> It is the cry of every human soul: "Where is the way?"

This is a sincere and good question Thomas is asking. And in a sense, it is the cry of every human soul, the soundtrack of our music and our movies and our activism and our religion. Where is the way? Only unlike Thomas, we are often unwilling to receive the answer.

But Jesus' response to Thomas—the question-asker, the seeker, the one who hears things and rolls them around his mind until he can process them—is a stunning declaration, perhaps the most important and most controversial words ever uttered in human history:

"I am the way, the truth and the life. No one comes to the Father except through me." (John 14:6)

This is the meaning of Easter. There is not a path or a principle. There is only a Person. Jesus is the way. Jesus is the truth. Jesus is the life. He didn't merely point to the truth. He didn't merely show them the way. He didn't merely tell them how to improve their lives. He's the end of the journey, the object of our obsessions, what our hearts truly long for.

✦ "My Lord and My God!" ✦

In that same room, days after Jesus' death, the disciples gathered, trying to make sense of what they'd just experienced. Mary Magdalene had just interrupted their gathering with the news that the tomb of Joseph of Arimathea, where Jesus was buried, was empty. What's more, she told them, or shouted really, "I have seen the Lord!" Peter and John had confirmed her story about the empty tomb. Now they all believed her. Somehow, Jesus was alive. Did they fully understand what this meant? No.

Then Jesus entered their midst. The door was locked for fear of being caught by the angry religious leaders and accused of stealing Jesus' body. But Jesus appeared anyway. You have to imagine they rubbed their eyes a bit. Was this real? "Peace to you!" He said. Reading their doubts, He urged them to see for themselves: "Touch me and see, because a ghost does not have flesh and bones as you can see I have" (Luke 24:39). And He asked for a piece of fish and ate it. A ghost doesn't eat a piece of fish. "Why are you troubled?" He asked, before explaining to them how this—His being alive and resurrected from the dead—was in fulfillment of all the Scriptures. The scales from their eyes began to fall off. They all believed.

Well, not all. There was one disciple missing. While ten of the twelve had gathered that evening, Thomas was not present. We don't know why he wasn't there, but we can guess that he was despondent. Thomas, the one who always got the facts and based his decisions on clear, rational thinking, saw the entire foundation for his faith come crashing down. Jesus was arrested by the Roman authorities, falsely accused, and unjustly crucified. How could He be so powerless as to let this happen? How could He be the Son of God? Had Thomas been duped? Was all of this a mirage? How could he have been so stupid? Perhaps he couldn't face the others with his shame and guilt and embarrassment. Maybe he didn't want to see the other disciples.

But it seems the disciples wanted to see Thomas. This is what good friends do. They were evangelists now for the message that Jesus was indeed alive. More than that, they knew that the best way for Thomas to work out his doubts was in community.

"We've seen the Lord!" they said, but he wasn't having any of it. The pain was too deep to believe another fantasy.

"If I don't see the mark of the nails in his hands, put my finger into the mark of the nails, and put my hand into his side, I will never believe" (John 20:25).

Russ Ramsey writes of Thomas's ultimatum:

For a man belonging to a people who had taken the name of a God they had never seen, based on covenant promises that same God had made hundreds of years before, Thomas knew the dangers of blind faith. What good was the hope of freedom when he lived in a land ruled by godless tyrants? What good was faith in a God who was living and active when the best candidate for the Messiah he had ever seen was arrested and put to death by God's own people?"[2]

Thomas was unmoved. But his friends loved him still. They did not give up on him. And a week passed, a week of conversations. A week of laughing and crying and reminiscing over all the good times they'd shared together. A week of breaking bread together.

Those hurting and doubting need our presence more than they need our propositions. And Thomas's road back to faith began with a simple nudge from his close friends. We love you. We care about you. Let us show you something. One atheist-turned-Christian writes of her conversion: "No one could have in a billion years of their gripping testimony or by showing me a radiant life of good deeds or through song or even the most beautiful of books brought me to Christ. I had to be tapped on the shoulder."[3]

We don't know what was said in those times, but we do know at the end of this week they were together again, in that same Upper Room. You have to imagine that they gathered in this space on purpose. Buildings don't hold any spiritual value, but places can be sacred. They can at times remind and draw us to certain spiritual moments of significance. Perhaps they thought that if they came back here, Jesus would appear, and Thomas would see Him. It's interesting that yet again they locked the doors. Though they believed, they still had some doubts and fears, as all of us do, even if we've been with Jesus for a while.

And as they gathered there, Jesus once again appeared, again the locked doors not a barrier for the Son of God. Jesus, reading Thomas's doubts, showed him His scars. "Stop doubting and believe" (John 20:27 NIV). Jesus wants Thomas to know that he's reached the end of his quest. The answer to our doubts is not a set of principles, but the sight of a Person, Jesus Christ, the Son of God.

Like a good shepherd, He meets His struggling disciple where he is, carefully tending to his soul. Thomas, who had said he'd only believe if he could touch Jesus' physical body and see the evidence for the resurrection, saw the doors of his heart opened, and he fell in worship. This was the Good Shepherd bringing home a lost sheep.

Thomas's words became a powerful declaration of faith: "My Lord and my God!" (John 20:28). This Jesus was no failed prophet or disillusioned revolutionary. To Thomas, it is clear that Jesus is both Lord of Creation and God of the Universe. But more importantly, Thomas is not content with mere knowledge and belief. Jesus, he declares, is *my* Lord and *my* God. This is the truth Thomas would be willing to go "die with him" for. And so it is this Easter, this is the truth that animates our worship. D. A. Carson writes that "Thomas thereby not only displays his faith in the resurrection of Jesus Christ, but points to its deepest meaning; it is nothing less than the revelation of who Jesus Christ is. The most unyielding sceptic has bequeathed to us the most profound confession."[4]

> Thomas's story shows us the paradox of Christianity: it is both faith and facts, believing and seeing.

This confession is really the only legitimate response to an encounter with Jesus. If it is true that Jesus rose from the dead, that the scars He bore on Calvary are still the scars He bears today, then we have no other option than to look at Jesus as "our Lord and our God." Thomas's story shows us the paradox of Christianity: it is both faith and facts, believing and seeing. Our faith is grounded in a mountain of historical facts that Luke describes in Acts as "many convincing proofs" (Acts 1:3), some of which another former skeptic, the Apostle Paul, lays out in 1 Corinthians 15. Scholars through the ages have come away unable to explain away, without intellectual dishonesty, Jesus and the movement He created. This book's purpose is not to offer the overwhelming evidence for Jesus' resurrection, but I highly recommend you read books like Strobel's *The Case for Faith* or N. T. Wright's *The Resurrection of the Son of God.*

And yet Jesus is not inhospitable to those who doubt, those who seek earnestly for the truth. Thomas stands in a long and illustrious line of those whose journey of faith began with questions. David, Abraham, Habakkuk, Jeremiah, Paul, Mary, the mother of Jesus, and even Martha and her complaining. And throughout church history, those who come with their honest questions and are willing to accept what or, more to the point, *Who* they find at the end of their quest, find faith. C. S. Lewis, Lew Wallace (author of *Ben-Hur*), Lee Strobel, and so many others. Thomas's words recorded in the Bible are few, but the questions he asked opened the door to some of the most powerful statements in all of Scripture: Jesus' declaration that He is the way, the truth, and the life, and Thomas's heartfelt "My Lord and my God!"

And even after we follow Jesus, we will still have questions. Questions are a sign of humility that there is a big God whom we can't possibly fully comprehend with our finite minds. Jesus visits those weak in faith, like the centurion who prayed, "I do believe; help my unbelief!" (Mark 9:24).

Jesus is beckoning doubters to come and see, to look at the facts of His resurrection and His proof of His deity, but more importantly to answer His summons to hope and joy and forgiveness and grace. I think right now of the beautiful hymn that has stirred the hearts of so many pilgrims and brings wanderers back home:

> *Softly and tenderly Jesus is calling*
> *Calling for you and for me*
> *See on the portholes*
> *He's waiting and watching*
> *Watching for you and for me*
> *Come home, come home*
> *You who are weary come home*
> *Earnestly, tenderly Jesus is calling*
> *Calling, "O sinner, come home."*

I can't even type these words without tears coming to my eyes. There is a bit of Thomas in all of us, walls of hurt and pain that fuel our doubts and fears. But Jesus turns to us with His scars, the wounds on His body that was beaten for us and says to us, "Peace be with you." In a sense, this is what we do every time we gather together for the Lord's Supper. This is what we are doing this Good Friday. We are pulling each other from despondency and despair back to the body and blood of Christ. We are reminded anew of His love for us.

And I want to end this chapter with an appeal to you, the reader. I don't know what circumstances caused you to pick up this book. Perhaps a friend gave it to you. Perhaps you found it in a bookstore. Or maybe you ordered the wrong item on Amazon. But I do know that your encounter with the risen Jesus on these pages as seen through the eyes of Thomas is no accident. So as you read, would you examine, would you look, would you see Jesus?

If you are a doubter, like Thomas, take heart that many more like you have walked this pathway home. If you are a wandering prodigal, know there is a welcome mat in the kingdom of God for your return.

Thomas, tradition says, not only was a believer, but became an evangelist to India and established churches there until he died as a martyr. And thus we see the power of the resurrection to change lives. Merrill Tenney says, "Thus belief in a risen Christ made a mourner into a missionary, a penitent into a preacher, the bereaved friend into an apostle of love, a timid and shrinking coterie of disciples into the fearless heralds of a new movement, and a doubter into a confessor."[5]

What, we are invited to ask this Easter, will the resurrected Jesus do, through us?

Study Questions:

◆ Consider the common myths about Thomas. Why do we only remember him for his doubts?

◆ Meditate on Thomas's bravery. Are you willing, like Thomas, to say, "Let's . . . die with him"?

◆ Review the reasons why Thomas may have been disillusioned after Jesus' death.

◆ Ponder Thomas's need to see Jesus' scars and see the physical resurrection.

◆ How has Thomas's inquiries helped solidify the story of the resurrection throughout church history?

◆ Ask yourself: Are my questions and doubts legitimate or are they sinful? Can I bring my doubts to Jesus?

Suggested Hymns and Songs:

There Is a Fountain—William Cowper
The Nail-Scarred Hand—B. B. McKinney

CHAPTER SEVEN

The Religious

The Pharisees, Scribes, and Sadducees

*No wonder the Herods, the Caesars and the Sadducees of this
world, ancient and modern, were and are eager to rule out all
possibility of actual resurrection. They are, after all, staking a
counter-claim on the real world. It is the real world that the tyrants
and bullies try to rule by force, only to discover that in order to do
so they have to quash all rumors of resurrection, rumors that would
imply that their greatest weapons, death and deconstruction,
are not after all omnipotent.*[1]

N. T. WRIGHT AND MICHAEL BIRD

*He answered them, "Isaiah prophesied correctly
about you hypocrites, as it is written:
This people honors me with their lips,
but their heart is far from me.
They worship me in vain,
teaching as doctrines human commands."*

MARK 7:6–7

I f there is a villain in the gospels, an Easter antagonist, it has to be the religious group known as the Pharisees. They seem to be always showing up and always on the wrong side of Jesus. You don't have to even go to church to not like Pharisees. They are useful stand-ins for every hypocritical person you've ever met, a convenient foil for our spiritual pride.

Most of us probably don't even know who these people really were, but that doesn't keep us from not liking them, not wanting to be them, or, horror of horrors, imagining ourselves a Pharisee. Our artists have satirized and popularized them, among them the late Charlie Daniels, who in one of his songs called them the "self-appointed sin patrol."[2]

This is probably the way most of us think of the religious leaders in Jesus' day, people against any kind of fun, who spent their downtime thinking up more rules and regulations. It gives us comfort that on Easter, we will dress up in our finest knowing that we would never, ever be this kind of person.

The truth is, much of what we think we know about the Pharisees and their religious adversaries, the Sadducees, is incomplete at best. What's more, as we look at their role in the Easter story, we will probably find more of ourselves in them than we'd like to admit. It could be that it's us walking into church with the spirit of the people in the Easter story we are most likely to despise.

✦ A Short History of Israel and the Priests ✦

The Pharisees take up the most ink in the gospels, but they were not the only religious leaders. Scribes and Sadducees also play an important role. Understanding them helps us better understand Easter.

In chapters 4 and 5, we saw some of the history of God's people who lived in Judea up to the first century. But it's worth revisiting, if only to understand how the various groups formed in response to political and cultural changes.

To get us there, we need to first take a tour through the way Israel's religious leadership developed. Throughout Israel's history, priests came from the family of Levi, Jacob's son, and from the family of Aaron, Moses' brother (Num. 3). By the time David became king, there were two families of priests in the Aaronic line: Abiathar and Zadok. Abiathar, however, was disloyal to David and conspired with rebels overthrowing his government, while Zadok remained loyal. Abiathar's descendants were cut out of this honor and Zadok's family continued to serve in the priesthood, even through all of Israel's history as a nation and well into exile under various world powers. At times, the priest held both a religious role and a political role, answerable only to the king or ruler over them. This lasted until about 174 BC, when the Seleucids, a Greek dynasty ruling Judea, took over the priesthood and appointed their own priests.

Secular control of the religious rites was part of the Greek rulers' program to assimilate Jewish people. At times they stripped Jewish people of their ability to worship according to their traditions and even killed many in order to enforce this. Eventually the Maccabees revolted, overthrowing their rulers and seeking to purify the priesthood after its defilement by the wicked king Antiochus Epiphanes. This victory against oppressors is memorialized in the Jewish holiday Hanukkah.

The new rulers during Israel's independence, the Hasmonean dynasty, were neither descendants of Levi nor Aaron, but nevertheless served as both kings and priests, a violation of the Levitical law and something that caused King Saul to lose God's blessing on his kingship (1 Sam. 13). Eventually the Romans conquered Judea and Herod the Great killed off the last Hasmonean high priest.[3] Now the priesthood would be under the control of Rome, chosen by whoever ruled Judea.

Jewish people reacted differently to these developments. Some accommodated themselves to power and welcomed assimilation into Greco-Roman society. Others resisted power and separated themselves from the culture.

✦ The Sadducees ✦

Among those most willing to work with the Romans and accept the cultural shifts were the Sadducees. As a result, the Sadducees were among the elite members of society and held a majority on the Sanhedrin, the powerful seventy-member ruling religious council given great deference in civil and legal matters. The chief priests Annas and Caiaphas were Sadducees appointed by Herod. In many ways, they were out of touch with the common people and were tolerated but not well loved. Sadducees, especially those in power, had to deftly navigate their relationship both with Rome and the people they were supposed to serve.

Interestingly, while they were liberal in their approach to power and culture, the Sadducees were ultraconservative when it came to the Hebrew Scriptures. They only accepted the five books of Moses, commonly called the Pentateuch. They also denied a belief in resurrection from the dead and most supernatural things like angels and miracles. They didn't believe in life after death. For Sadducees, the temple was the center of worship and life.

✦ The Pharisees ✦

The Pharisees were the ideological opposites and political adversaries of the Sadducees. Pharisees sought a renewal movement in Israel through obedience to God and good works. They resisted Roman rule and sought to separate from Greco-Roman culture. Pharisees were also the spiritual leaders of the common people, often teaching in their synagogues across Israel. They were revered as religious figures.

Pharisees saw themselves as steadfast guardians of the moral and spiritual traditions of the Jewish people. They scrupulously adhered to the Scriptures, both the Torah and the writings of the prophets. They also held up their oral traditions that interpreted the Scriptures as authoritative, an ever-growing series of laws and regulations to ensure the purity of their people. Unlike the Sadducees, they believed in the resurrection of the dead, in miracles, in angels, and in life after death.

✦ The Scribes ✦

The scribes were closely aligned with the Pharisees, with whom they are often linked in the Bible. This was a class of scholars whose job it was to know, study, and copy and recopy the Hebrew Scriptures. This required a devotion to detail. Scribes were well regarded as knowledgeable scholars and teachers. When Jesus, as a twelve-year-old boy, is found conversing with the teachers in the temple, He is likely engaging with scribes (Luke 2). One of the reasons the scribes were so opposed to Jesus was because His teaching seemed to replace them. Those who heard Him said He spoke as "one who had authority, and not like their scribes" (Matt. 7:29).

✦ Jesus and the Religious ✦

The scribes, Pharisees, and Sadducees all opposed Jesus, but for different reasons. The Sadducees didn't believe in resurrection and sought to disprove Jesus' belief in the afterlife, trying to trap Him with a question about marriage in the afterlife (Matt. 22:23–32). Jesus was ready, pointing them back to their sacred texts, to the very law of Moses they held as the only authoritative source, and the book of Exodus specifically, where God tells Moses at the burning bush, "I am the God of Abraham and the God of Isaac and the God of Jacob" (Mark 12:26). God was declaring that He is currently the God of the patriarchs who had gone before. "He is not the God of the dead but of the living" (v. 27).

Why would Jesus be a threat to the Sadducees? On one level, Jesus' teaching about the kingdom of God and the resurrection, His performance of miracles, and the movement growing behind Him could stir up the people in ways that might threaten their power. The Sadducees thrived in keeping the status quo. If that equilibrium was upset, the Empire, ever alert to unrest, would rouse and turn its gaze on Judea. The Sadducees did not wish to poke the bear and so worked hard to maintain a fragile peace. The Sadducees couldn't afford another uprising and another brutal crackdown by Rome. This would eventually come in AD 70 as Titus destroyed Jerusalem, and the Sadducees lost power and influence for good.

But it wasn't just the faint echoes of insurrection they seemed to hear in Jesus' words. Jesus' moral teachings also encroached on their turf. It was one thing for this itinerant Galilean to take His show across Israel and gather crowds to listen to His teachings and see His miracles (which they refused to accept). It was quite another for Jesus to come calling in Jerusalem and to expose their temple racket, where they exploited the poor and where they held almost absolute power.

The temple was everything to the Saddu-cees. Their chief priests ruled with an iron fist, cleverly navigating the Roman political system and maneuvering into positions of authority and prestige. Annas, the retired high priest, pulled the strings from behind the curtain, and Caiaphas did what was in his own best interests. It was these men to whom Judas came with the offer of Jesus for thirty pieces of silver.

> Everyone tiptoed around the corruption in the temple, but Jesus wasn't afraid.

Everyone tiptoed around the corruption in the temple, but Jesus wasn't afraid. He violated their sensibilities, too, when Jesus declared that one day this magnificent temple would be destroyed, with not a single stone left upon another (Mark 13:2). Jesus was a threat to them, which is why they sought to kill Him. Of course, this treachery violated the law of Moses, but they'd offer Jesus up on trumped-up charges of insurrection and insufficient loyalty to Rome. This gambit worked, forcing Pilate's weak hand. The chief priests knew that the shaky ruler couldn't afford another revolt. Pilate would authorize Jesus' execution, and their hands would be clean.

But they thought they had killed the Jesus movement when they killed Jesus. And yet after Jesus' resurrection, the Sadducee leaders pan-icked at the reports from the elite Roman guards chosen to guard Jesus' tomb that His body was gone and the tomb was empty. Instead of investigating whether Jesus rose from the dead, they plotted to cover it up. Matthew's gospel records them bribing the guards to spin a story that the disciples—the very scared men who ran away and were locking themselves in a room in fear—suddenly found the courage to steal Jesus' body (Matt. 28:11–15). And after Pentecost, when those men suddenly were empowered by the Spirit to preach on the reality of Jesus' resurrection, the same religious leaders sought to put a stop to the Jesus movement again.

Luke records the angst of the Sadducees: "They were annoyed that they [the apostles] were teaching the people and proclaiming in Jesus the resurrection of the dead" (Acts 4:2). The resurrection always seems to annoy, especially those who, like the Sadducees, fear the reality of a resurrected Christ. Like so many today, they had staked their worldview on the material and the temporal, so a risen Jesus, an inaugurated kingdom, and a new creation were not welcome signs of hope and liberation, but the end of their ability to build their own little kingdoms of exploitation and greed. A risen Jesus creates an alternate community, an outpost of another kingdom, and glimpses of a new world coming, one that makes right the injustices of the world and empowers the weak and feeble of this world. This is scary for Sadducees, both ancient and modern.

Jesus presented different problems for the Pharisees, with whom He may have been more aligned. Unlike the Sadducees, whom they despised for their corruption, greed, and accommodation of the Greek culture and Roman power, the Pharisees considered themselves a renewal movement. New Testament scholar N. T. Wright describes their motivation:

> The Pharisees, due to their political marginalization in the Herodian period, became largely concerned with manufacturing the conditions necessary for Israel's eschatological restoration through a strict regime

of Torah observance as seen from within their specific tradition. In other words, they were not a separatist religious club. Rather, they were a Jewish renewal movement, seeking to draw Israel towards the conditions that would hasten its restoration before God and its elevation over the surrounding nations. The Pharisaic agenda, then, was to purify Israel by summoning the people to return to the true ancestral traditions; to restore Israel to its independent theocratic status; and to be, as a pressure group, in the vanguard of such a movement through the study and practice of Torah. The Pharisees aimed to demonstrate, in the present time, that they were the ones whom Israel's God would vindicate when, as expected, he acted to rescue his people.[4]

So you see, it's not just that they were cranky old men whom nobody would invite to parties and who dreamed up more ways to make people miserable with more petty rules. The Pharisees were concerned with the renewal of God's people. They took seriously the words of the prophets who warned God's people about idolatry and sin. They earnestly believed that personal purity and obedience to the law would hasten God's promise of the coming kingdom. In many ways, if the Sadducees were the liberals skeptical of the supernatural and cozy with the culture, the Pharisees were the conservative, Bible-believing faithful who worked for spiritual and cultural renewal.

This is why we often misinterpret Jesus' clashes with the Pharisees. Too many Christians think of Jesus as a freewheeling hippie who blew off the importance of purity and God's good law in favor of a laissez-faire approach, and the Pharisees as the out-of-touch law keepers. But this is not really what the gospels are telling us.

Jesus wasn't against spiritual renewal. He, after all, delivered the Sermon on the Mount which stressed the goodness of the law, urging an even stricter adherence to it:

"You have heard that it was said, Do not commit adultery. But I tell you, everyone who looks at a woman lustfully has already committed adultery with her in his heart." (Matt. 5:27)

But while the Pharisees thought they could muster up the righteousness to make themselves good in order to see God's kingdom come, Jesus' message was that the righteousness and purity could not come from outside, but from within. Even the most devout amongst them would fail to see the kingdom of God:

"For I tell you, unless your righteousness surpasses that of the scribes and Pharisees, you will never get into the kingdom of heaven." (Matt. 5:20)

Consider what Jesus said to the most fastidious law keeper of his day, Nicodemus: "Truly I tell you, unless someone is born again, he cannot see the kingdom of God" (John 3:3). The Pharisees were right to desire renewal and to long for the coming of the kingdom of God. They were right to be scrupulously devoted to the law of God. But their obsession with purity became a kind of self-righteous moral improvement, with an ever-increasing list of demands of the oral tradition that they held on the same level as Scriptures. Their self-righteousness was taking them further from, rather than closer to, God, and Jesus quoted back to them Isaiah's rebuke:

"So for the sake of your tradition you have made void the word of God. You hypocrites! Well did Isaiah prophesy of you, when he said:

"'This people honors me with their lips,
but their heart is far from me;
in vain do they worship me,

> *teaching as doctrines the commandments of men.'"*
> (*Matt. 15:6–9 ESV*)

"Teaching as doctrines the commandments of men." This was legalistic self-righteousness. In contrast to the Sadducees, who were corrupt and elitist and aligned with the culture and the state, the Pharisees saw themselves as the more spiritually pure. This is why they were incensed that Jesus, as a rabbi and teacher of the law in the same synagogue where they'd teach, would dare to be seen with the same people who the Pharisees saw as compromisers and sinners whose impurity would slow the coming of God and invite His judgment (Mark 2:15–17).

Their self-righteousness was taking them further from, rather than closer to, God.

This is why Jesus' story of a Pharisee praying in the temple and in his prayer, contrasting himself with a tax collector and saying, "God, I thank you that I'm not like [that person]" (Luke 18:11) would be a common occurrence. The contrast was intentional. They wanted to show God that they were not as impure and unrighteous as their compromising neighbors.

For the Pharisees, Jesus had a word. It was the sinner, the tax collector, the impure one who was actually closer to God. Not because it was virtuous to violate the law, but because he understood his inability to make himself pure. Like the Pharisees, Jesus was concerned with the kingdom and the law, but He pointed out where they had missed what else the prophets had said: A new day was coming when there would be rebirth in the people of God. Joel, Ezekiel, and others called for a day when change would come from the inside. This was the whole subtext of the Old Testament Scriptures. Underneath the judgment of God's people for sin and idolatry was the promise that a new king would arise who would first suffer (Isa. 53). The ritual sacrifices and traditions that the Pharisees so zealously and carefully followed were all leading to something: the final Lamb of God who takes away the sins of the world (John 1:29; Heb. 10:1–18).

Jesus affirmed the goodness of the law (Matt. 5:18). And He was more zealous for spiritual purity and rebirth than the Pharisees. But He diagnosed the problem with their program. What the people of God needed was not mere self-improvement and earnestness, but to be changed from the inside:

> *"And no one puts new wine into old wineskins. Otherwise, the wine will burst the skins, and the wine is lost as well as the skins. No, new wine is put into fresh wineskins." (Mark 2:22)*

This is why John's ministry of baptism was so offensive to the religious elite. Why would Jewish people need to repent and be converted if they were already the people who were right with God? Jesus came on the scene and announced that the kingdom was already in their midst. He called for repentance, even for the religious. And He urged a people known for their love of the Scriptures and who "search the Scriptures" to see that they all point to Him (John 5:39 esv). Jesus, by way of the cross, was the renewal movement they were looking for. He would atone for the sins of those who believe and send the Spirit of God to regenerate their hearts and tune them towards obeying the will of God.

Many Pharisees rejected Jesus and were on the Sanhedrin and in the crowd that urged the Romans to crucify Jesus. But there were others who listened, including Nicodemus. And later a former Pharisee named Saul had his own encounter with Jesus and would write much of the New Testament.

✦ You, Me, and Easter Pharisees ✦

So on Easter, we see two diametrically opposed groups of religious leaders find common cause in opposing Jesus; Sadducees because they saw Jesus' claims of deity, His talk of resurrection and kingdom, and His dismissing of the temple as a threat to their hold on power; and Pharisees because they saw Jesus as a threat to God's coming kingdom reign, an assault on their desire for spiritual renewal. And His declarations of who He was, not just God's representative but the very Son of God, one with the Father, were blasphemy in their ears. It was primarily the Sadducees who moved the levers of power to convince Pilate and the government to crucify Jesus, but it was the Pharisees who were among the crowd shouting for His execution.

> Nobody has clean hands at Easter.

The mistake would be to read the gospels and look askance at these Jewish sects, sure *we* would be among the small group of people who heard and believed Jesus' words. Too many, in fact, have read the Bible throughout Christian history and have come away with this conclusion, even leading to anti-Semitism. But the Christian gospel tells a different story. New Testament scholar Tom Schreiner writes, "The very point of the story is that if the leaders of God's people, who knew the OT promises of salvation from reading the Scriptures, executed Jesus, then there is no people group anywhere at any time that would have done otherwise."[5]

Truthfully, nobody put Jesus on the cross. Jesus went willingly, accepting the cup of God's wrath, standing down the armies of heaven, refusing to defend Himself for one purpose: to lay down His life for the sins of His people. More importantly, He died for you and He died for me. Jesus' unjust trial and crucifixion is the fulfillment of God's promise given well before the formation of the Jewish nation in the Garden of Eden, that out of Eve would come a redeemer who would crush the head of the serpent (Gen. 3:15). And it's a former Pharisee, Paul, who would write that the entire world, every ethnic group, stands condemned before God because of sin (Rom. 1). And yet the good news, that Christ has paid for this sin and offers reconciliation with God, is available to all peoples (Matt. 28:19–20).

In a sense, we all put Jesus on the cross, because each of us, across every ethnic group and social class, stands condemned before a holy God. Nobody has clean hands at Easter.

I don't know where you are this Easter as you read this book. Perhaps you picked up this book with a sophisticated indifference toward the supernatural in a world that looks skeptically at resurrection and Jesus' divinity. Or maybe you arrived with a healthy sense of your own self-righteousness, proud of the way you've been a good person, a good citizen, a good husband, a good mom, sure you are better than your vile neighbors and more sinful family members. You might even feel good because you try to go to church as often as you can, and you recycle, support all the right hashtags on social media, and give money to your favorite charities. We can be so busy, like the Pharisees, separating ourselves from those we perceive to be morally upside-down that we forget the sin in our own hearts.

Jesus has a word for you, whether you feel good or bad at Easter, whether you consider yourself a saint or a sinner, a pagan or a preacher. Most of us probably have a bit of Sadducee and Pharisee in us. We carry some bit of embarrassment about the claims and demands of that first-century Galilean *and* a healthy sense of our own moral rightness. Today it's even possible to be a Pharisee about not being one of those Pharisees. But the good news is that Jesus has a message for all of us who just maybe exhibit a tiny bit of self-righteousness from time to time: Come to the Father.

In the parable of the Prodigal Son, told to a crowd of Pharisees, Jesus invited the religious to find redemption. He told a story of a prodigal, the kind of moral reprobate the Pharisees knew would be far from God's kingdom. But He also told the story of another kind of prodigal, one who was striving to do all the right things to please the Father but whose heart was also on a far journey. To the listeners of His day, it would be scandalous for God to offer forgiveness and grace to a son who had so dishonored the Father; and yet to us it might seem scandalous that God would offer that same grace to those who don't think they need it. But this is what Jesus is doing.

Tim Keller says this of Jesus: "He is not a Pharisee about Pharisees; he is not self-righteous about self-righteousness. Nor should we be. He not only loves the wild-living, free-spirited people, but also hardened religious people."[6]

What marvelous good news this Easter! Jesus went to the cross for the very Pharisees who didn't think they needed salvation. He died for the skeptics and Sadducees, both ancient and modern. He conquered sin and death so that those who believe could experience the kingdom of God and personal spiritual renewal. And His resurrection means that both skeptics and saints, Sadducees and Pharisees, can find salvation and become part of a new family made up of the formerly self-righteous from every nation, tribe, and tongue. It means that we—recovering Pharisees—find grace.

STUDY QUESTIONS:

- Think through the common perception of Pharisees in today's culture and how different they are from what we really know of these religious people.

- The Pharisees were concerned with moral and spiritual renewal and waited for the kingdom of God. These are good motivations. So where did their quest go wrong?

- How can religious people miss Jesus?

- Explain the difference between Pharisees and Sadducees.

- How did the Sadducees accommodate themselves to power? Why were they so intent on destroying Jesus?

SUGGESTED HYMNS AND SONGS:

Grace That Is Greater Than All Our Sin—Bart Millard
At Calvary—William R. Newell

CHAPTER EIGHT

The Witnesses

The Women at the Tomb

A virgin gave birth to Christ; a woman proclaimed that He had risen again. Through a woman death, through a woman life.[1]

AUGUSTINE

So the women were terrified and bowed down to the ground. "Why are you looking for the living among the dead?" asked the men. "He is not here, but he has risen!"

LUKE 24:5–6

In my book *The Characters of Christmas,* we explored the unusual way God announced the birth of Jesus to the world. The news that the Son of God, both divine and yet human, was entering the world He made was not first delivered through couriers to Caesar Augustus in Rome or the sycophants in Herod's palace or even the faithful scribes who pored over every jot and tittle of the law. Instead, an angelic chorus filled the sky above tiny Bethlehem and heralded the news of Jesus to common shepherds, those who were close to the ground, who tended sheep sacrificed for Passover and could be trusted to bear the news of the coming of the Lamb of God.

So we should be no more surprised that the announcement of the second entrance of the Son of God into the world, the miraculous re-emergence from death, the bodily resurrection of Jesus would also be announced in an unconventional way. This time, no angelic chorus appeared. A single angel on the tomb told five ordinary women that it had happened: the event that all creation since Eden had been groaning for in anticipation.

Today it may not seem so strange that women were the first to see the empty tomb of Jesus or that women were the first ones to announce the empty tomb to the rest of Jesus' followers. But in the first-century Greco-Roman world, women were not the messengers the world would trust to bear important news. Women were not trusted as witnesses in a court of law, in the court of public opinion, in important deliberations.

And yet the gospels all record women beholding and telling, seeing and sharing, weeping and waiting as the promise of salvation history, whispered by the Almighty to a woman back in the garden, came to fruition that Sunday morning. It wasn't Pilate, the feckless governor who allowed the injustice of Jesus' death to happen, or the Apostles who fled in fear, or the Roman guards who fainted as death suffered its final blow and the scarred but whole body of Jesus was raised to triumphant life. Commentator Leon Morris lauds their courage: "Against the background of the failure of the male disciples the devotion and the courage of the women shine out."[2] No, it was this band of women, unremarkable, who discovered the most important square footage in all of human history, the empty space that fills human hearts.

✦ Mary(s) Did You Know? ✦

Who are these women we see on the pages of history on the day the world changed? Matthew says that there were "many women" who witnessed the death and resurrection (Matt. 27:55–56), but at least five are named by the gospel writers. This kaleidoscope of perspectives, rather than disproving Jesus' resurrection, adds additional detail and a layer of witness testimony to the miracle. Each woman came to this moment in history with her own story, an ordinary person swept up in God's story of redemption.

Joanna

She came to Jesus from an unlikely place. Unlike the others who followed Him, she was close to royalty. Her husband, Chuza, held an important office in Herod Antipas's government. But her proximity to power, her access to the finest care in the world, couldn't help her troubled body and soul. She would find healing in an unexpected place, in an encounter with her fellow Galilean, the traveling rabbi carpenter with nowhere to lay His head. Only Luke records her name in two brief, yet important mentions. First, describing Jesus' ministry in Galilee, it is Luke who emphasizes the inclusion of women in the growing band of disciples:

> *Afterward he was traveling from one town and village to another, preaching and telling the good news of the kingdom of God. The Twelve were with him, and also some women who had been healed of evil spirits and sicknesses: Mary, called Magdalene (seven demons had come out of her); Joanna the wife of Chuza, Herod's steward;*

*Susanna; and many others who were supporting them from their
possessions. (Luke 8:1–3)*

It was not unusual for a rabbi to have disciples. It was expected.
What was unusual was for a rabbi to include women among his followers. New Testament scholar Leon Morris writes what a norm-breaker
this was: "The rabbis refused to teach women and generally assigned
them a very inferior place. But Jesus freely admitted them into fellowship, as on this occasion, and accepted their service."[3]

Jesus, preaching the good news of the gospel of the kingdom, em-
bodies the gospel of the kingdom by raising the status of women, so
often belittled and kept down by the sinful structures. Luke seems to
indicate that Joanna experienced some kind of physical healing. We
don't know what ailment she suffered from, but we can imagine that
her husband's position in the palace afforded her the opportunity to explore the best medicine of the day without success until she met Jesus'
healing hand. And some scholars think that her husband is the royal
official in John 4:46–47 who comes to Jesus pleading for healing for his
dying son: "Sir, come down before my boy dies" (v. 49), he begs Jesus.
A man with means—in stature, power, and money—begs the traveling
rabbi to use His healing powers to bring his son to life. John records
that by the time the Roman official returns from Cana to their home in
Capernaum, the boy had made a miraculous recovery. Could it be that
this is the family of Joanna? Did their family experience two miracles?
We don't know, but we do know that in desperation Joanna—insider,
connected, powerful—was brought to her knees and to Jesus' feet.

Luke records the legitimacy of her faith. She was following Jesus
and supporting the mission financially (Luke 8:3). Salvation had

touched her body, her soul, her heart. The grace she was so undeservedly given she freely dispensed for the mission of Jesus.

Joanna's life is an example of desperation, surrender, and service, but it also shows us the diverse and countercultural kingdom of Christ. Joanna didn't really belong among the mix of disciples, both because she was a woman but also because she was part of a despised insider ruling class, a dysfunctional and corrupt palace. Remember it is this Herod who had John the Baptist murdered for daring to call out his adultery (Matt. 14:3–10). And yet where it seems the message of Christ might least likely take root, in this insulated, ungodly place, is the very place where the gospel had its healing work, even inviting the intrigue of Herod himself (Luke 23:8).

> In desperation Joanna — insider, connected, powerful — was brought to her knees and to Jesus' feet.

Think of this for a moment. Herod, the powerful son of Herod the Great who tried in vain to kill baby Jesus (Matt. 2:16–18), cannot escape the kingdom of God encroaching on his own house, first with close associates believing in Jesus, and then standing face-to-face with Jesus at His trial.

Joanna's story reminds us that God seeks and saves in the least likely of places, that God's light shines in the most hideously dark places. I'm reminded of this when I am in places like Washington, DC, a symbol of power and often corruption and self-dealing. I am amazed at the presence of Christian witness all over the government, in both parties. We too easily write off people for their ideological positions, as if God only saves people that think like we do. Jesus' revolutionary band brought people from across the spectrum, from zealots who wanted to overthrow Rome to tax collectors who preyed on their fellow citizens to insiders in Herod's palace. And so it is today, that the kingdom of God touches down in the homeless shelter and the halls of power, in prisons and palaces, slums and corporate board-rooms. Jesus saves paupers and politicians, presidents and pawnbrokers, partyers and the pious. Resurrection power is not limited and, even today, breathes life into dead souls where we least expect it.

Mary Magdalene

Jesus appeared *first* after His resurrection to Mary Magdalene. But when she met Jesus it was she who was a sight to behold, afflicted, Mark's gospel notes, with not one, not two, but *seven* demons (Mark 16:9). Most of us who live in a heavily Christianized West have probably never encountered anyone afflicted with demon possession, but those who have traveled to more pagan countries tell stories about how the evil spirit world can prey on the hearts of those who have succumbed to their power. Seven demons is Mark's way of telling us that if anyone in the world was considered hopelessly imprisoned by severe affliction, it would be Mary. We don't know exactly how seven demons affected Mary, but it's likely that she exhibited severe signs of mental illness and uncontrollable rage.

> While the religious men sought to kill Jesus, frail, troubled Mary Magdalene believed.

Imagine Mary's life before Jesus. Hopeless, forgotten, destitute. Who hires someone with seven demons? And yet she, like Joanna, met the healer, the Lord of Creation, the only one whose word the demons must heed. Few of us can imagine the desperation that brought her to the Master. Out of options, out of hope, out of resources, she fell at Jesus' feet and found healing.

It's interesting to me that Mary Magdalene is so central a figure in the Easter story. While the religious men sought to kill Jesus, while the scribes pored over the Scriptures, while the Romans dismissed the movement as fringe, the frail, troubled Mary Magdalene believed.

Mary's story should encourage us, because the least likely to become a central figure in the greatest story ever told became the first one to tell it. First to meet Jesus at the empty tomb. She had come there in the dark and couldn't believe her eyes. She'd witnessed a lot in the three years with Jesus: opened eyes, healed limbs, even bodies raised from the dead. She had heard Him promise to be killed and then rise again. But to be there and gape in at the empty husk of a grave, silhouetted against a dark night sky was something else altogether. So she runs weeping to the disciples, barely able to spit out the words, "They've taken the Lord," she wept. It was personal. He was *her* Lord. Taken by . . . them.

But on her return trip, she heard a voice, a recognizable whisper. "Mary," the resurrected Jesus said softly. I read these words in John 20 and can barely contain the emotion, goose bumps forming and a lump rising in my throat. Jesus called her name. What a moment. And so it is for everyone who calls Jesus their own. It isn't just Mary's name He whispers, but but yours and mine when we look up and behold the risen Christ.

It's incomprehensible, really, that this woman—she of seven demons, trouble, sorrow, and ill repute—would be the very first evangelist on the very first Easter. And yet in many ways it makes sense when seen through kingdom eyes. Jesus takes the desperate, the afflicted, the enslaved, and transforms them into witnesses of His glory.

Mary (Mother of Jesus)

What can you say about Mary and what she must have suffered? Oh, she had known this day was coming ever since the angel Gabriel gave her the stunning news that she'd carry the Christ child in her womb, ever since the old man in the temple, Simeon, spoke over the Christ child those haunting words directed toward Mary: "A sword will pierce your own soul" (Luke 2:35). She felt that pain, kneeling at the foot of the cross, as her son was pierced in His hands and feet and a Roman sword knifed into His side. She watched as the one she raised, taught to speak and walk, hung on an ugly piece of timber, whipped beyond recognition, crying out in agony, gasping for His last breaths. In a way, Jesus' pain was her pain in the way all mothers feel when their children suffer. What hurt her more, the physical lashes to His beloved body or the cruel mockery of her innocent son? And yet she knew that Jesus also made her pain His pain, bearing her own sin, carrying her suffering on His slumping shoulders as He finished the work He came into the world to do.

Mary would be there at the cross while everyone left. Mothers do this. When the friends disappear, when the hangers-on stop hanging on, when the crowds filter back to their homes. Mothers stay long after the lights are off and the glory fades. Mothers sit in prison cells and at bedsides and on desperate late-night calls. Mary did what mothers do. And so much more. Only Mary would know what it is like to be mother to the Son of God, to know that Jesus was both her son and yet was God's son, both her precious child and yet the Savior of the world. Every parent has to let go, to release our children to the mission of God. Yet Mary had to unclasp her hands from Jesus in a most profound way. She watched, she listened, she wept.

So that morning as she made her way to the tomb, we don't really know what she was thinking. Was she recalling Jesus' prophetic words, the rumors of resurrection? Did she think that perhaps it could be true? What is clear is that Mary was there to visit the tomb of her son. What an awful, painful, necessary journey. Parents are not supposed to visit the graves of their children, and yet Mary epitomizes the pain of every parent who has lost a child. Mary also bears the promise of what awaits God's people at the end of the age. An empty tomb not only means Mary's Son is alive, but that every son and daughter who is in Christ will also rise again one day. Her son, the firstfruits of every son and daughter.

> Mary did what mothers do. And so much more.

The "Other" Mary and Salome

There were two other women named in the gospels who were part of this group that went to the tomb that Sunday morning. We know less about them, but their presence is no less important. There is another Mary. So that makes three Marys who were at the tomb. Mary seems to have been a popular name at the time, similar to Joseph and John and Judas. When I was writing this book, I jokingly texted my editor and wondered if we should commission an Easter song with the title: *Mary(s) Did You Know?* Mark Lowry, if you are reading this, you are free to steal my idea.

Matthew describes her as the "other Mary" (Matt. 27:61). Mark (15:40, 47) adds some more descriptive language and calls her "the mother of James the younger and of Joses [or Joseph]." Many scholars believe this is the same as the Mary, "wife of Clopas," mentioned in John 19:25 as standing at the foot of Jesus' cross. The name Clopas seems to be a Hebrew name for Alpheus. Their son James is mentioned as an Apostle of Jesus (Matt. 10:3; Mark 3:18; Luke 6:15; Acts 1:13).[4] The historian Eusebius, writing in the third century, said that Clopas/Alpheus was brother of Joseph, Jesus' father.[5] This would make Mary Jesus' aunt and the sister-in-law of Jesus' mother Mary.

There isn't much said in the Scriptures about this "other Mary," other than that she is present in the darkest moments of Jesus' life, standing there with the other women near Jesus' cross and there at the tomb as the first rays of light shone that Sunday morning. You'd expect this kind of loyalty, I suppose, from family members, from the mother of one of Jesus' closest disciples. Of course, we know that family doesn't always imply loyalty. Others in Jesus' family rejected and mocked Him. Mary stuck by Jesus when the disciples fled and everyone faded away. This is the nature of true friendship—often less about what we do and more about our presence in the midst of someone's grief. At the cross, at the grave, in there with those she loved. It appears her presence was so important that she was named in Matthew and John's gospel, her name written into Scripture.

The last woman named as a witness of Jesus' resurrection is Salome, the mother of James and John, the sons of Zebedee. Salome seems to be a fixture in Jesus' inner circle. She's the mother who, along with her husband, released her sons to leave their nets and follow Jesus (Matt. 4:21–22). Salome is the mother with the courage to ask Jesus if her two sons could have a prominent place in the kingdom of God (Matt. 20:20–21). Nicknamed the "Sons of Thunder" by Jesus, James and John were rough around the edges, once asking God to call down fire and punish the Samaritans (Luke 9:54). And yet this family meant a lot to Jesus. John was present there at the cross, receiving instructions on the care of Jesus' mother after Jesus' death (John 19:26–27). Salome released her children to the Lord, desiring that they be close to Jesus. She would see them both follow the Lord and become pillars of the early church. She'd suffer heartache and tragedy, enduring the tragic death of her son, James, who would later be executed by Herod (Acts 12:2). Her other son John would go on to live a long, full life, but would endure severe persecution and exile on the island of Patmos. Jesus answered her prayer for greatness for her sons, but fulfilled it in ways she couldn't have imagined back when the rabbi first called them "fishers of men."

✦ An Apologetic for Resurrection ✦

There is a deep significance that the first witnesses to the resurrection were women. It's significant in two ways. First, the gospels record a kind of unbroken chain of eyewitness testimony from the time of Jesus' arrest all the way through His resurrection, with names included that could be historically verified. New Testament scholar N. T. Wright, whose massive study *The Resurrection of the Son of God* is perhaps one of the most significant and exhaustive examinations of the evidence, remarks: "The women are prominent in all of the gospels: they saw Jesus die, watched his body being laid in the tomb, discovered the tomb empty and encountered an angel (or two)."[6]

Another scholar, R. T. France, concurs: "They are therefore the guarantee that when the tomb is found to be empty there has been no mistake: these same women saw him die and saw where he was buried; they would not have gone to the wrong tomb."[7] Richard Bauckham notes the "scrupulous *care* with which the Gospels present the women as witnesses"[8]—in particular, Matthew's account in which Mary, Jesus' mother, Salome, and "the other" Mary are named as present, from death to resurrection.

The Law of Moses required the presence of at least two witnesses to verify a story (Deut. 17:6), and yet the gospels not only say "many women" were present but names at least five! This is part of an overwhelming amount of circumstantial evidence Luke would later describe as "many convincing proofs" (Acts 1:3). Later Paul, the former skeptical Pharisee, would conclude after his investigation that over five hundred witnesses saw Jesus alive after His death (1 Cor. 15:6).

There is a second reason the testimony of the women is crucial to believing the reality of the resurrection. It's a counterfactual proof, but as we have seen, in the first century the testimony of a woman was not considered valid evidence. Justin Taylor and Andreas Köstenberger explain the way women in the first century were treated:

> In the first century, women were not even eligible to testify in a Jewish court of law. Josephus said that even the witness of multiple women was not acceptable "because of the levity and boldness of their sex." Celsus, the second-century critic of Christianity, mocked the idea of Mary Magdalene as an alleged resurrection witness, referring to her as a "hysterical female . . . deluded by . . . sorcery."[9]

So even though today, by modern standards of scholarship, the witness of these many women in seeing Jesus dying on the cross, buried, and then risen is a hard-to-refute piece of evidence for the reliability of the gospels and the historicity of the resurrection, the fact that women's testimony was not received in the first century is also another piece of evidence. Why? Because the gospel writers and the Apostles and disciples who gave their lives in response to Jesus' resurrection would not have put forward the inadmissible evidence of female witnesses if they were fabricating a story. They would not have built their story based on the word of women. In fact, we know this because Jesus' disciples didn't believe Mary Magdalene, Joanna, Mary, and the others. Luke says, "But these words seemed like nonsense to them, and they did not believe" (Luke 24:11). And N. T. Wright argues that this is why you don't see Paul name the women in his resurrection account in 1 Corinthians 15, because this would not be convincing to a first-century audience: "Clearly some even in the early days saw the presence as an embarrassment when announcing the gospel to a skeptical audience. Had the gospel stories been invented in the post-Pauline period, then, the likelihood of the women playing such a prominent role would be reduced to nil."[10]

But even more than serving as proof that Jesus did indeed rise from the dead, the presence of women at the cross, at the empty tomb, and as early and faithful evangelists in this new movement God was building in the church tells us something about the upside-down nature of God's new creation.

The empty tomb is Eden come full circle. The Bible tells us that Satan cast his dark shadows near that forbidden tree in the garden, exploiting the innocence of a woman and thus ushered in the curse of sin. In a world where death and destruction reign, sin, like a virus, takes malignant root in the human experience. Meant to live in compatible harmony, men and women would conflict, with men often fulfilling God's macabre prediction that "he will rule over you" (Gen. 3:16). In other words, men would use their strength, not in defense of women, not to protect women, not to build up women, but to put them down, sometimes through laws and strictures and often through violence.

Misogyny would not have and will not have the final word, however. For it would be through the offspring of a woman where God would move through human history to rescue His creation. The painful labor in childbirth, once a curse, would now birth the salvation of the world in Jesus, and it is to women that God would first announce that resurrection has happened and that death has been defeated. Women, essential for human existence, and the first messengers of God's new creation.

The empty tomb is Eden come full circle.

Christianity is saying that even though sin has pitted men against women, there is another day coming when men and women will be restored to their original, fully flourishing, side-by-side purposes. God has restored new creation patterns in Scripture, where men no longer use their strength against women, but in Christlike love lead empowered by the Spirit of the Second Adam. And women are empowered as heirs of Eve, heirs of those first witnesses, living out God's original, flourishing vision of womanhood. In the church today there is much conversation, some helpful, some harmful, about the role of women. But while we may disagree on the roles, we can agree that God often uses women as bearers of the good news of His resurrection around the world. The list is nearly endless of those who have, like Mary Magdalene, Joanna, the two Marys and others, shared the news of the gospel to skeptical audiences: Lottie Moon, Gladys Alward, Fanny Crosby, Henrietta Mears, Harriet Tubman, Catherine Booth, Rosa Parks, Dorothy Day, Mother Teresa, Joni Eareckson Tada, and so many more.

It's fashionable to see Christianity as repressive to women, judged by modern standards, but true students of history and Scripture understand how radical, how progressive the biblical vision of complementarity and mutual love laid out in Scripture really was for its time. Even the ways in which the church is often judged by her peers is rooted in an ethic about women that originated in the gospel story and spread throughout the world. God loves, values, and prizes women. And so should we.

This Easter, we honor the witnesses of the Easter miracle by listening to their words and believing that Jesus is not in that tomb but is ascended to the Father in victory over sin and death. Like Mary, we should listen to the voice of the one who says, "Why do you seek the living among the dead? He is not here, but has risen" (Luke 24:5–6 ESV).

STUDY QUESTIONS:

- Consider the significance of women being both witnesses of Jesus' crucifixion and His resurrection. How does this add weight to the evidence in favor of Jesus' resurrection?

- Consider the significance of God choosing women to be the first to share the news of Jesus' resurrection. What does this say about the way Christianity sees women?

- Consider the life of Mary Magdalene. How did her encounter with Jesus change her and what does her life say about the power of the gospel?

- Why is the presence of the empty tomb so significant to Christianity? How does this separate Christianity from every other religion?

SUGGESTED HYMNS AND SONGS:

Glorious Day—Casting Crowns
Is He Worthy?—Andrew Peterson

CHAPTER NINE

The Secret Disciples

Nicodemus and Joseph of Arimathea

The tomb that Joseph offered was not a final resting place, but rather the ultimate symbol of God's complete and final victory over sin and death and his delivery of the promise of forgiveness and new life to all who put their trust in him.[1]

PAUL TRIPP

"Are you a teacher of Israel and don't know these things?" Jesus replied.

JOHN 3:10

He prayed fervently every time his car approached a border guarded by antagonistic Soviet soldiers as he sought to enter a closed country, Bibles stashed in his belongings. "Lord, in my luggage I have Scripture I want to take to Your children. Do not let the guards see those things You do not want them to see."

Brother Andrew, known as "God's Smuggler," was responsible for sneaking millions of copies of the Word of God behind the Iron Curtain during the Cold War and helping plant the seeds of hope in places bereft of gospel witness, places ruled by a Communist government that restricted Christianity and persecuted Christians. Today his ministry, Open Doors, has a presence in sixty countries around the world and is continuing to advocate for persecuted followers of Christ.[2]

Today in the West, we enjoy the precious gift of religious freedom. In some places it is even popular to be called a Christian. It can get you an audience, a job, and book contracts. Politicians even claim Christianity in order to win votes. So it can be difficult for us to grasp what it means to have to keep our faith a secret. But let us meet two characters in the Easter story in whom secret disciples around the world might find inspiration. Nicodemus and Joseph of Arimathea were marginalized believers in a different sort of way. They enjoyed power and prestige among the religious elite—but had to keep their love for Jesus quiet.

✦ Nic at Night ✦

We know from the gospels that Jesus' ministry provoked mostly widespread opposition from religious leaders, both the Sadducees and the Pharisees, but the Bible shows us specific examples of religious leaders who earnestly sought to understand Jesus and eventually became followers of Christ. Of these, Nicodemus is perhaps the most prominent. We first meet him on the pages of John's gospel as he seeks out a meeting with Jesus at night and probes the itinerant teacher with a series of questions.

Imagine the scene here. You have the rebel rabbi who has been gathering crowds and rebuking the religious. Sitting next to Him, perhaps the most prestigious teacher in Israel, a devoted Pharisee who longed to see his people and his nation commit themselves to renewal and obedience to the law in order to usher in God's kingdom. Jesus had just ravaged the temple before Passover (John 2:13–17), whipping the exploitative merchants, turning over the money changers' tables, declaring that what should be a house of prayer had become a shameless bazaar for greed. He had declared that the temple was "his Father's house" and that one day a temple (His own body) would be destroyed and raised up again (John 2:16–19). Many Jews believed in Him but a good many others were angry, especially the Sadducees, who controlled the temple. He had shamed them—before Passover at that—calling out their true motives, and now they were bitterly opposed to Him. Nicodemus was a Pharisee but held a seat on the Sanhedrin, the prestigious, seventy-member ruling body dominated by Sadducees.

This was likely one reason for him to request a secret meeting with Jesus. John 3 describes him as a "man from the Pharisees" and a "ruler of the Jews." Perhaps he was sent to sit down with Jesus and find a way to make peace. Both Jesus and the Pharisees shared an affinity for God's law. Both believed in life after death and resurrection. Or perhaps he wanted to have a conversation away from the demands of the crowds and the distractions of the day. It is obvious from their dialogue that there is more going on. Nicodemus had observed Jesus from afar, seeing His miracles, witnessing the results of His healing power, and listening intently to His teachings. Nicodemus was clearly seeking. Was Jesus the long-promised Messiah, the one come to save Israel?

It is interesting how Nicodemus addresses Jesus. He calls Him "rabbi" and admits that Jesus is clearly a "teacher who has come from God" (John 3:2). Nicodemus was in awe of some of Jesus' miracles, saying, "no one could perform these signs you do unless God were with him." This is high praise from the most respected teacher of his day. Unlike other Pharisees, Nicodemus was unwilling to rule out these "signs" or explain them away as works of Satan. You can see the churn in his heart and mind: *God is up to something here.*

And yet, as close as Nicodemus came to understanding Jesus, he was still so far. Jesus got to the heart of Nicodemus' spiritual quest. "Unless someone is born again, he cannot see the kingdom of God" (John 3:3). Jesus understood the longing in every Pharisee's heart for the kingdom of God to come, for national renewal and God's righteous rule. But it wouldn't come through personal behavior and obedience to the law. Nicodemus—yes, the devout, wise, educated preacher and teacher—still needed conversion. His law-keeping, his religion, his rituals could not get him one step closer to the doorstep of the kingdom than if he had been a pagan. Yes, Jesus was telling Nicodemus, you too need something supernatural, something otherworldly, something outside of yourself in order to get into God's kingdom.

But Nicodemus, still in spiritual darkness, was willing to listen and probe, to ask and wrestle. "How can these things be?" he asks. The rabbi and teacher, who often answered these kinds of questions from His own disciples, was now the student. Jesus became the superior teacher, the scholar to this scholar, speaking with authority only heaven could grant.

It's easy to question why Nicodemus came to Jesus at night, away from the crowds. Those of us who have never faced any opposition for our Christian faith, who probably have more fish stickers on our cars than we do unbelieving friends, might not get what it is like to live as a Christian in a desperately hostile Christian environment, but we would be foolish to consider Nicodemus a coward in this moment. Even to meet with Jesus at night was an act of courage, a willingness to obey that small echo of faith. To be seen with Jesus carried with it enormous risk for such a prestigious religious leader. The Pharisees would soon cast off anyone from their synagogue if they professed faith in Jesus (John 9:22), something Jesus would later warn His disciples of in His Upper Room discourse (John 16:2).

Jesus never rebuked Nicodemus for his slow, secret quest. R. C. Sproul says this is in keeping "with our Lord's refusal to put out a faith that, being mingled with fear, seems to be a smoldering wick (Isa. 42:3)."[3]

We should be thankful for this smoldering wick, for Nicodemus' probing questions of Jesus inspired for us perhaps the most beautiful words in all of Scripture: Jesus' declaration of His mission, words that the Spirit of God has blown into the hearts of people in the millennia since their fateful encounter on a warm Jerusalem night. "For God loved the world in this way: He gave his one and only Son, so that everyone who believes in him will not perish but have eternal life" (John 3:16).

By these words, many smoldering wicks, many Nicodemuses have met Jesus in their own dark nights of the soul and have emerged as children of the light. Jesus' words are both a declaration and an offer—a declaration that religious works cannot paper over a dead heart, and an offer to believe in the one who is not only a teacher but a Savior.

> Jesus never rebuked Nicodemus for his slow, secret quest.

We don't know if Nicodemus converted that night, but he shows up again in John's gospel (John 7:50–51), defending Jesus in what seems to be a private discussion among religious leaders. The Pharisees were angry that Jesus had declared Himself to be "living water" at the Feast of Tabernacles, a sacred rite that commemorated God's faithfulness to them in the desert (Lev. 23:42–43). Jesus invited the Jewish pilgrims in Jerusalem that day to believe in Him and find "streams of living water," a fulfillment of the prediction by the prophets of the coming of the Holy Spirit (Isa. 55:1; Joel 2:28). His claims of deity caused some to believe but also caused many Pharisees to be enraged at what they considered blasphemy. Nicodemus urged them to resist a rush to judgment on Jesus' deity, reminding them that the law required them to do their due diligence.

Again we don't really know the state of Nicodemus's faith at this point. Was he still a seeker just pleading for a full hearing for Jesus? Was he speaking of his own journey, of his own personal investigation of the claims of Christ? We cannot say. But it shows courage here to stand up to the crowd enduring scorn and insult. Months later, Jesus would not get a fair hearing from the very ruling body, the Sanhedrin, that Nicodemus served with such distinction.

✦ "A Good and Righteous Man" ✦

In the Christmas story, we meet an unknown man named Joseph who helped care for Jesus in His birth; and in the Easter story we meet another unknown man named Joseph who helps care for Jesus in His death. Joseph of Arimathea shows up in every gospel account of Jesus' death. He is described by Matthew as a "rich man" and a "disciple of Jesus" (Matt. 27:57–60). Mark describes him as a "prominent member of the Sanhedrin" and someone who was "looking forward to the kingdom of God" (Mark 15:42–46). Luke calls Joseph "a good and righteous man," a "member of the Sanhedrin" who didn't agree with their decision to seek Jesus' death (Luke 23:50–51). John called him a "disciple of Jesus" who kept his faith secret due to fear of his fellow religious leaders (John 19:38).

Joseph's hometown was the Judean village of Arimathea, a town in the hilly region of Ephraim, twenty miles northwest of Jerusalem. Some scholars think this could have been the same hometown as that of Samuel, Israel's celebrated prophet and priest.[4] The gospel writers are clear that Joseph, like Job, was known for both his integrity and his wealth. This is a good reminder to us that riches and righteousness are not always mutually exclusive. God often calls the poor and ignoble of this world, but that doesn't preclude Him from calling wealthy Christians to use their means for the kingdom of God. Joseph was one of those men. Like every faithful Pharisee, he was looking for the kingdom of God, but Mark's gospel tells us that while many of his peers found that "kingdom" in obedience to the law and personal piety, Joseph saw in Jesus the fulfillment of those kingdom promises. But he had to keep his allegiance to Jesus a secret as a member of the Sanhedrin.

♦ Two Against the Crowd ♦

The lives of Nicodemus and Joseph converged as they became unlikely actors in God's redemptive drama. These two had a lot in common as Pharisees on a Sadducee-dominated Sanhedrin. Pharisees were minorities among Israel's elite leadership but were the majority sect among the people. So imagine how Nicodemus, Joseph, and other Pharisees on the council must have winced at the elitism of their peers and fought for the voice of the people among the corruption and self-dealings of the leadership class. Pharisees resisted the worldliness of the Greco-Roman culture and loathed their Roman occupiers. They wanted Israel to live up to its calling by God to be a distinct people. They eagerly awaited the kingdom of God and the resurrection at the end of the age. The Sadducees were much more sophisticated, preferring accommodation with the Romans, even purchasing power through corruption and backroom deals. They held the seats of power, including the chief priest roles. And they rejected belief in miracles and the afterlife.

But it was Jesus who would bring Nicodemus and Joseph even closer. To believe in this itinerant rabbi and His claims to be the Son of God put them at odds even with their Pharisee brethren. We can't imagine the wrestling in their souls as they straddled their identity as proud Pharisees and the tug of the Spirit on their heart as they investigated the claims of Jesus. Unlike many, they seemed to "search the Scriptures" (John 5:39 ESV) and see Jesus on every page, bursting out in the predictions of the prophets. How they must have (unobtrusively) watched the miracles, seen the demon-possessed suddenly find peace, witnessed the lame leave their mats and walk, and finally been convinced. These two men, strong in integrity and righteousness, could not escape the conclusion that would put them at odds with their synagogue, their families, and their community.

But how providential of God to have Nicodemus and Joseph find each other. We can imagine the hallway conversations and the late-night sessions discussing Jesus. And we can then imagine the terrible discomfort each would feel as Jesus was arrested and stood trial before their august body. Did they push back among the seventy other members of the Sanhedrin? Did they reiterate Nicodemus's plea that his fellow religious leaders resist the rush to judgment and the mob justice and give Jesus a fair hearing? Luke tells us Joseph disagreed with the decision, but how strongly did they voice it, and were they silenced?

What anguish Joseph and Nicodemus must have felt both as disciples of Jesus and members of the very body that would send Jesus to His death. How powerless these two powerful men must have felt! And what they couldn't know and didn't yet understand was that Jesus' march to the cross was not really the work of the Sanhedrin. The Son of God wasn't the pawn of the corrupt power brokers, but rather the seemingly powerful leaders were used by God to bring about His plan of redemption and their salvation.

✦ Secret No More ✦

Somewhere between the trial before the Sanhedrin and Jesus' crucifixion, Joseph of Arimathea and Nicodemus made a decision to take their private faith public with an extraordinary gesture. Perhaps exhausted by the long days, disillusioned by their fellow Pharisees' embrace of injustice, or grieving over the loss of the one upon whom they'd rested their messianic hopes, they decided to give Jesus in His death what Israel refused to give Him in His life: acknowledgement as King. So Joseph requested permission from Pilate, the Roman governor, to take the body of Jesus off the cross. The bodies of all three who died by crucifixion that night—Jesus and the two insurrectionists who died alongside Him—would be removed, because Jewish leaders requested that the bodies not hang on the crosses overnight in violation of the law. Their deaths were hastened by the breaking of their legs to eliminate their ability to lift themselves up and find breath. Jesus, however, died many hours sooner, and His legs didn't have to be broken. Instead, they pierced His side, confirming He had succumbed.

Joseph's request caught Pilate by surprise. Jesus was dead sooner than he expected. Perhaps Pilate was relieved that this Jesus problem was finally taken care of. But he was probably even more surprised to see a member of the Sanhedrin standing before him, willing to risk position and reputation to give Jesus a king's burial.

This is what Joseph and Nicodemus are doing here. Typically a criminal would be dumped into an empty grave or pauper's field, buried ignominiously under a pile of rocks.[5] So this was highly unusual, both that Pilate granted their wishes and for them to so publicly identify with an enemy of the state, one convicted of treason and insurrection.

There were a lot of important considerations here for Joseph and for Nicodemus and for the women who accompanied them to the burial of Jesus. First, this act was their way of giving Jesus, in death, the respect as King of the Jews that He didn't receive in His life. He would be buried not in an empty field but in a rich man's tomb, fulfilling the words of the prophet Isaiah (Isa. 53:9).

It was important for them to not only get the body off the cross, but to bury Jesus quickly before sundown and the start of Sabbath on Passover week, when work had to cease. Joseph's tomb made sense as a burial spot, likely near Golgotha where Jesus was crucified but outside the city walls.

Both Joseph and Nicodemus did this at great sacrifice—Joseph giving up his tomb and Nicodemus paying for costly burial spices and ointments. John 19:39 says it was seventy-five pounds, an extraordinary amount, reminiscent of Mary of Bethany's extravagant display of washing Jesus' feet with expensive ointment. Bible scholar Merrill Tenney describes the burial process:

> The Jews did not embalm as the Egyptians did, by removing the soft organs of the body, and by drying the muscular tissues with preservatives. The corpse was washed (Acts 9:37), and swathed in bandage-like wrappings from armpits to feet, in the folds of which spices were placed (Matt. 27:59; Luke 23:53), and a cloth was wound around the head.[6]

This was a difficult task, peeling Jesus' bloody body off the cross and carrying Him the distance to the tomb, body fluids still dripping. They had to carefully wrap Him in the bandages and anoint His body with both the myrrh as a preservative and the aloes and perfumes to minimize the stench of decomposition. This was an act of love for Joseph and Nicodemus. Two high-ranking religious officials, stooping low and exhausting themselves to honor their Lord. You imagine their friends, their families, wondering why these two men of stature would take such care for a rejected Messiah, a despised enemy of Rome. And as they performed this thankless task, racing daylight to get Him into Joseph's tomb before sunset, doubt and fear crept into their hearts. What would their lives look like next? If Jesus was God, how could He allow Himself to be arrested by the Sanhedrin and crucified by the Romans? Why didn't He summon the armies of heaven and fight back?

> Their private faith — the secret they whispered to each other in the halls of Jerusalem — would now be public.

What they did know was that their private faith, the secret they whispered to each other in the halls of Jerusalem, would now be public.

Nicodemus and Joseph didn't realize that Calvary did not spell the end of Jesus, but the end of death. The blood-encrusted body they laid in that tomb would soon come to life, shaking off the cloth wrappings and thus the chains of death. Nicodemus couldn't have known that the expensive embalming ointments and perfumes used to give Jesus a King's burial were only temporary. Joseph didn't know that his fresh-cut tomb would only be a temporary resting place for the Son of God. This grave would sit empty forever, and so would the graves of those who know Jesus as Lord. Joseph's prized real estate would stand as a witness of Christ's triumph over the curse of sin. I've had the opportunity to visit Israel several times and see the two sites where it's possible Jesus was buried. Both graves are empty.

The worst night of their lives, when darkness seemed to envelop the world, became the dawn of something new.

✦ The Gift of the Grave ✦

It's easy for us to wonder why Joseph of Arimathea and Nicodemus were so quiet about their faith. We imagine ourselves having more courage by being more open with our faith. But I think this perspective is unfair and shortsighted. Courage looks different on different people and in different situations. At times Jesus did not speak or move about openly, knowing His enemies sought Him but His time had not yet come. There are situations where prudence is the best witness, such as Christians in closed countries, working to slowly plant seeds of gospel witness, or Christians in prominent leadership roles, who must weigh their words in order to steward their influence. This isn't always cowardice. Sometimes we need a Dietrich Bonhoeffer faith, willing to suffer death for our convictions, and sometimes we need a Brother Andrew faith, stealthily working underground to advance God's mission.

This is hard for us to comprehend in an age when we think every thought has to be expressed all the time on every medium. Public proclamation is important, but so is the need to "seek to lead a quiet life" (1 Thess. 4:11) and to be "quick to listen, slow to speak, and slow to anger" (James 1:19). Their courage showed up when it was most necessary and not a moment too soon.

What's more, the inclusion of Nicodemus and Joseph of Arimathea in the Easter story shows us how God works in mysterious ways to accomplish His purposes in the world and the gospel's power to work in the most surprising places. The Sanhedrin seemed the last place to find disciples of Jesus. Even as the kingdom of God was moving among the poor and the outcast, it was also moving among the powerful, in the very councils that wrote His death sentence, pinpricks of light in a dark world.

Some of the most important evidence for Jesus' resurrection would be gathered by the members of the very body that sent Him to the cross. They both saw Him physically dead, a lifeless corpse leaking blood and water. And they buried Jesus in a prominent place where nobody could mistake the miracle, so much so that Jesus' enemies had to bribe the Roman soldiers assigned to guard Jesus to lie about it (Matt. 28:11–15).

God used Nicodemus and Joseph in creating the most important apologetic of the Christian faith. Without the empty tomb, we are, to quote Paul, "of all men most miserable" (1 Cor. 15:19 KJV). The secret disciples, by their quiet acts of faithfulness, shouted the good news of God's redemptive love to the world.

Study Questions:

- Consider Nicodemus and Joseph of Arimathea. What would they have to give up to publicly declare their faith in Jesus?

- Reflect on the journey of Nicodemus from devoted and respected teacher to follower of Jesus.

- Reflect on the generosity of Joseph of Arimathea. What compelled him to offer his tomb as a proper burial place for Jesus?

- Meditate on the courage of both of these men in standing up to the Sanhedrin in defending and following Jesus.

- Ask yourself: in what areas of my life am I willing to go against what is popular in order to follow Jesus?

Suggested Hymns and Songs:

Because He Lives—Bill and Gloria Gaither
The Old Rugged Cross—George Bennard

CHAPTER TEN

The Executioners

Who Were the Romans?

The amazing initial (and enduring) reflex of Jesus' crucified heart was to forgive. This is amazing, astounding grace![1]

R. KENT HUGHES

Then Jesus said, "Father, forgive them, because they do not know what they are doing." And they divided his clothes and cast lots.

LUKE 23:34

One of my father's favorite scenes from the Easter story, one that would often bring to tears a man who rarely showed emotion, is the scene in which the Roman soldiers, following Judas, sought Jesus. "Who is it that you're seeking?" Jesus asked. John 18 records the soldiers' response, "Jesus of Nazareth," to which Jesus replied, "I am he." This response of Jesus declaring Himself to be the eternal "I am" caused a detachment of men from the greatest fighting army at the time, representing the world's undisputed superpower, to fall back in fear at the power of Christ.

I suspect Dad loved this scene so much because it's a microcosm of the Easter story, the clash of both heavenly and worldly powers. This man from Nazareth, the carpenter's son, born in a cave in a backwater village, had more strength in His words than the world's mightiest army wielded in all their weaponry.

You can't really explore the Easter story and understand its characters without understanding Rome and the Romans. They lurk in the background of the gospels, not quite center stage. The Romans, who ruled the known world at the time of Jesus, were used by God to create the setting in which the Son of God was born and died to save sinners. Paul, both a proud Roman citizen and an observant Pharisee-turned-Christian who would one day be executed by the Romans, would tell the believers at Galatia that Jesus' entrance into the world came "when the fullness of time had come" (Gal. 4:4 ESV). Scholars Andreas Köstenberger, Scott Kellum, and Charles Quarles offer three reasons why this time in world history was the perfect moment for Jesus to enter the world:

- ✦ Two hundred years of world peace, secured by Roman military strength, allowed the spread of the Christian gospel.
- ✦ Romans built a network of highways that stretched throughout the empire, enabling easy travel. It is in the towns along these roads that churches were planted.
- ✦ The conquests of Alexander the Great, prior to Roman rule, made Greek the language of commerce throughout the Roman Empire. This provided a common idiom that became a universal vehicle for the spread of the gospel.[2]

This time in which Jesus was born, lived, and died was established and set in motion largely by the Roman Empire. So what should Christians know about the Roman Empire to help us understand the story of Easter?

✦ The Global Superpower ✦

So what was the world like in the time of Christ? For one thing, it was dominated by Rome. Rome is often referred to as an Empire because that's exactly what it was. It would be hard to travel anywhere in the known world that wasn't ruled by Rome. At its peak the Empire stretched from "Britannia" in the west to Armenia and Mesopotamia in the east. They were the world's sole superpower, dominating with the world's most disciplined fighting force. What's more, in the first century, the entire Empire was experiencing what historians call the *Pax Romana,* a time of peace. Of course, this peace was the costly result of Roman might savagely crushing the opposition in a series of brutal civil wars. The emperor at the time of Jesus' birth, Octavian (Augustus), had declared himself Emperor, and Rome became less of a Republic and more of an Empire. The Roman Senate deified Augustus and his successor, Tiberias. This meant that the Emperors were seen not merely as leaders, but gods to be worshiped as divine.

Rome was an extremely religious—or superstitious—society. When Roman rulers conquered a nation, they made a practice of incorporating local religions and deities into the pantheon of gods of Rome, to which were added the Greek pantheon of gods. Citizens were expected to participate in the sacred rituals to the gods, both publicly and privately. And there was no such thing as a concept of "separation of church and state" like we might experience today in the West. Religion and rule were intertwined. "Political leaders wanted peace and security, and 'religion' was one vital way to achieve that. This is why emperors built temples, sponsored religious rites, often attempted to reform religious practices, and sometimes even enforced participation in religious observances by whole cities," write scholars Michael Bird and N. T. Wright.[3]

And yet as pluralistic as it seems Roman religion was, it wasn't necessarily tolerant. There was a social expectation for Roman citizens to participate in the religious rites. Bird and Wright note: "Failure to observe commonplace piety, like attending great festivals or adhering to certain specialized rules such as those concerning the vestal virgins, could result in severe penalties."[4]

For the people who lived in Israel, religious toleration was complicated. Given the volatile history of the region, in which her various conquerors tried in vain to extinguish Jewish religious rites and practices, the Roman government had learned, often the hard way, to offer the Jewish people a bit of autonomy, as long as they were faithful Roman citizens, paying taxes and obeying the laws. At times, the expectations of Rome and of the Jewish people clashed, such as the time Pilate insisted on having his soldiers enter Jerusalem displaying Roman symbols, resulting in violent unrest. Pilate eventually backed down. However, Rome still held ultimate authority, appointing Israel's high priests. It was easier for Romans to tolerate Jewish religious practices because they included so many festivals and rituals. Later, when Christianity emerged, it was more difficult to understand because it emphasized a religion of the heart and worshiped a God that could not be seen in any meaningful sense. In fact, Christians were called atheists and accused of cannibalism because of their practices of the Lord's Supper. Most Jewish people at the time of Christ detested the pagan worship in Rome. Jewish belief in

> As pluralistic as Roman religion was, it wasn't necessarily tolerant.

monotheism—the existence of one God—set them apart from other Roman subjects.

For faithful Jews, seeing the symbols of Roman power, the flag flying high above Jerusalem, was a painful reminder of what they had lost: their independence and their national identity. So while some in the religious elite accommodated themselves to this new reality, many longed for the day when a Messiah would lead them out of captivity and victory over the Romans.

The heavy Roman taxation was another galling reminder of their powerlessness. Punishing levies took much from the average citizen of Jerusalem and, to make matters worse, Rome often employed Jewish mercenaries to collect these taxes and at times charge a steep commission on top of it.

Though Rome was very powerful and wealthy, not all Roman citizens enjoyed the benefits. The Empire was divided into several classes of people, ranging from the wealthy political and aristocratic elite all the way down to the working-class poor and the many slaves from countries Rome had conquered.

What united Romans and Jews and almost every other subject society in the Empire was a common language. Before Rome conquered the known world, Alexander the Greek had Hellenized the world, making Greek the common language and enabling widespread commerce between city-states and the ability of disparate people groups to communicate with each other. It's likely that Jesus and the disciples mostly spoke Greek. The Bible they read was the Septuagint, the Greek translation of the Hebrew Old Testament.

✦ Jesus, Caesar, and Us ✦

What's interesting is the way the gospel writers describe Jesus' interactions with the Romans. His appeal and popularity grew out of the fact that He was performing miraculous deeds and fulfilling the words of the prophets for a coming Messiah. To many Jews, this kindled hope that perhaps the one who would finally usher in spiritual renewal and lead Israel in victory over the dreaded Romans was finally here. And yet every time Jesus had an opportunity to achieve political victory, He resisted, infuriating His followers, to the point where He withdrew to the mountain because He perceived that the crowd wanted to "take him by force to make him king" (John 6:15).

At times Jesus even seemed to acknowledge the power of Caesar. He was once approached by Pharisees and Herodians about paying taxes. Pharisees resisted assimilation to Roman culture, urging the Jewish faithful to be a distinct people in order to usher in spiritual renewal and the kingdom of God. Herodians were quite the opposite, accommodating and assimilating to Roman power. Both had perverse motives for trapping Jesus with this question of the tax. If Jesus said to pay the taxes, He would be betraying the majority of Israel, the Pharisees, who detested Roman power. And yet if He resisted the tax, He'd run afoul of the Roman government, thus encouraging the kind of insurrection against Caesar that the Herodians and Sadducees eventually accused Him of fomenting in their arguments urging Pilate to execute Him.

Jesus' response satisfied neither group, but gives us a window into the future relationship between the church and the state. "Give to Caesar the things that are Caesar's, and to God the things that are God's"(Mark 12:17).

In this statement, Jesus acknowledged Caesar's power to tax and the responsibility of God's people to submit to civil governments. Paul would later echo this same advice in Romans 13, when urging Christians to pay their taxes. And yet Jesus also was being quietly subversive. There are certain things owed to Caesar—the tax—but Jesus was

> **Jesus would be a subversive, but not an insurrectionist.**

saying that Caesar is not owed everything. In other words, as much as he is worshiped, the emperor is not sovereign over all the universe. Caesar, Jesus is saying, is not God. And so you don't owe everything to a temporary ruler. He is both urging God's people to obey their governments, and yet reminding them that these rulers are temporal and ultimately powerless before God. Jesus would be a subversive, but not an insurrectionist.

◆ The Roman Who Believed ◆

In perhaps the most famous encounter with a Roman soldier, recorded in Matthew 8 and Luke 7, Jesus made a statement that would provoke anger and shock among Jewish people. Jesus was in Capernaum, a thriving port on the Sea of Galilee, where He had met and called Simon Peter, James, and John and where He spent much of His ministry. He was approached by a Roman centurion with a desperate request. One of his servants suffered from paralysis and apparently lived with excruciating pain.

Typically, Roman soldiers were hated by the Jewish people. They were often deployed to quash protests or even put to death enemies of the state. It would be Roman soldiers who would not only arrest Jesus but execute Him. They represented the power of the state, the occupying army that symbolized Israel's subservience. And yet Luke says that *this* Roman soldier was different. He was a God-fearing Roman, enjoying a stellar reputation among those he ruled.

A centurion commanded a company of around a hundred men. He was powerful, and yet we see him on his knees before a poor Jewish teacher, begging for a miracle. It illustrates the limits of the power of Rome and reminds us that the real power in Israel was in the God-man whose words could bring healing and life.

The centurion didn't come to Jesus arrogantly. He could have ordered Jesus to perform a healing. He could have used his troops to kidnap Jesus and hold Him hostage until he got what he wanted. He could have assumed that Jesus owed him a miracle because of his status, barking, "Do you know who I am?" And yet, this man humbles himself and begs Jesus on behalf of his servant.

Jesus gives this man his miracle. But He does more than this. He holds up as a role model this Roman soldier, the symbol of everything every faithful Jew would hate about their occupiers, and says, "I have not found so great a faith even in Israel" (Luke 7:9).

Think for a moment about what Jesus is saying here. The greatest demonstration of faith was not coming from one of His disciples. It was not coming from the religious leaders. No, the greatest demonstration of faith, in Jesus' eyes, came from a member of the hated Roman army, the one whose actions would support a bloodthirsty empire, a member of a cohort that would one day arrest and crucify Him on behalf of a corrupted state. This man, according to Jesus, had the greatest faith in all of Israel.

Jesus is demonstrating here the power of the gospel and the central story of Easter. Listen to His words:

> *"I tell you that many will come from east and west to share the banquet with Abraham, Isaac, and Jacob in the kingdom of heaven. But the sons of the kingdom will be thrown into the outer darkness where there will be weeping and gnashing of teeth" (Matt. 8:11–12).*

The gospel, Jesus is telling the people of Israel, is not just for Israel, but for the whole world. What's more, we will be surprised who we see around the table in the kingdom of God. Those who seemed the furthest from the kingdom of God because of their outsider status and their sins will be in heaven because of their simple faith in the one who would pay for their sins and reconcile them to God. And those who seemed closest to God because of their outward religious practices and all the cultural boxes may they've checked not be in heaven because they never showed the simple faith of this centurion.

But this was not just a message for pious Jews in the first century. It's a message for religious people everywhere. God finds faith where we least expect it. Those who seem so far from God—those we have been trained to hate and despise—may have more faith than those of us who think we are close to God. Jesus' own band of disciples included both zealots who wanted to overthrow Rome (Simon) and tax collectors sympathetic to Rome (Matthew). There was room for both resisters and accommodationists.

> We should ask ourselves this Easter who we think is unreachable, who seems beyond Jesus' love.

What's more, the gospel is not just for a certain group, but for the whole world. We should ask ourselves this Easter who we think is unreachable, who seems beyond Jesus' love. And then we should repent, for in excluding someone from Jesus' saving love we might be guilty of limiting the gospel. Jesus' death and resurrection would make it possible for sinners anywhere to come humbly to the cross and beg for mercy as this centurion did. And in Christ, God is building a multiethnic body, drawing believers to Himself from across cultures and ethnic groups and socioeconomic classes. *This* is the story of Easter.

✦ **Killing Jesus** ✦

Over the centuries since the first Easter, the question has been asked, "Who killed Jesus?" The answer is both complicated and simple. It's complicated because from an earthly perspective, there were many responsible for Jesus' unjust death: the religious leaders hell-bent on seeing Jesus eliminated for either blasphemy or because He was a threat to their power; Pontius Pilate, who had neither the power nor the will to preside over a just trial; and the Roman soldier, who actually carried out this state-sponsored death.

And yet if we understand the true story of Easter, we recognize that nobody really took Jesus' life. He offered it freely for the sins of His people (John 10:18). And the Father, before time began, determined that the Son would die as a substitute to atone for the sins of those who believe (Isa. 53:10). Moreover, the human responsibility for Jesus' death is shared by all sinners. All of us have gone astray, the prophet Isaiah says, and the Lord has laid on Jesus all of our sins (Isa. 53:6). God made Jesus to be "sin for us," Paul would later write in 2 Corinthians 5:21, "so that in him we might become the righteousness of God."

But the actual task of carrying out Jesus' death did fall to the Roman soldiers, on command from Pontius Pilate. I've often wondered how these men felt as they whipped Jesus to within an inch of His life, hoisted Him up on the stout wood post, nailed His wrists and ankles, and stuck the sword deep in His side to prove He had died.

The gospels give us a bit of a glimpse into how these soldiers might have felt. We see two scenes that remind us just how ordinary it was for Romans to execute criminals arrested for insurrection—the charge against Jesus. Crucifixion was a uniquely Roman practice, designed for a slow painful death and maximum indignity to dissuade future insurrectionists. For many of the soldiers this was just another day at the office, as they gambled below the cross for a piece of Jesus' garments (Matt. 27:35–36). We don't really know what this practice meant, other than a macabre game to pass the time and offer further embarrassment to the one being crucified. We also hear the mocking words of some soldiers: "Hail, king of the Jews!" (Matt. 27:28).

The irony of this scene is rich. These soldiers didn't know what they were saying. The Son of God could have commanded legions of angels and had these hardened men of war flat on their backs. He could have marshaled the power of God and resisted His arrest. But He yielded to the way of the cross so these men who mocked Him might have salvation. If Jesus did come down from the cross, no one would ever be able to ascend up to Heaven and know God.

Yet Jesus, even as He suffered in agony, whispered forgiveness toward His captors, "Father, forgive them, for they do not know what they are doing" (Luke 23:34 NIV). These Roman soldiers were mere pawns in a long cosmic battle between the seed of the woman and the seed of the serpent (Gen. 3:15). This is true of every human being, laden with sins we choose and sins we commit without knowing, the human heart so wicked we don't even know the depths of our depravity.

And yet at this cross, at Easter, we can find forgiveness in the death of the Innocent One.

Not all of the soldiers mocked. One soldier, a centurion, looked up at Jesus and declared, "Truly this man was the Son of God" (Matt. 27:54). Was this a statement of belief in Jesus as the Son of God? Or was this an acknowledgment, after the ground split open and the sky turned dark, for this Roman soldier that Jesus was more than a mere man, perhaps divine? We don't know, but we do know that not every heart at the foot of this cross was hardened. Some were able to look up and believe.

We might wonder if this Roman centurion is the same person visited by Peter in Acts 10, a believer who desired the filling of the Holy Spirit and by whom the gospel would begin to spread among the Gentiles. Perhaps this is the same person, or perhaps this centurion told other centurions, and the gospel ran like wildfire through the Roman garrison.

And this would not be their last encounter with Jesus. Days later as they were guarding the sealed tomb where Jesus was laid, soldiers again were confronted with the I Am, pushed flat on their backs and unconscious as the Son of God shook off the shackles of death and rose from the grave:

> *There was a violent earthquake, because an angel of the Lord descended from heaven and approached the tomb. He rolled back the stone and was sitting on it. His appearance was like lightning, and his clothing was as white as snow. The guards were so shaken by fear of him that they became like dead men. (Matt. 28:2–4)*

The soldiers were bribed by the religious leaders to keep this on-the-ground report of a man's rising from the dead to themselves, but could they have possibly kept that promise for long, after what they saw?

✦ The Kingdom of God ✦
and the Kingdoms of Men

In the end, the Roman Empire went the way of every earthly empire, into the dustbin of history. Today you can tour the vestiges of Roman power—the architecture and symbols that still exist in Western Europe. And much Roman influence still holds sway over our systems of law and justice across the world.

Yet the movement that emanated from the man the Romans put to death on that Judean hillside still stands, as the church of Jesus Christ thrives around the world. Two thousand years later, followers of Jesus gather in storefronts and caves and cathedrals and homes around the world declaring that Jesus, not Caesar or any other ruler, is King. Caesar may have been worshiped as divine, but ultimately Roman power faded into obscurity while the real King of the Universe was the one bloodied and beaten, whose power came not from human ingenuity and military might, but from God.

This Easter, we are reminded that no matter what our situation, we can trust ultimately the power of God over human systems both just and unjust. And we are reminded that Jesus was saving, calling, wooing the very people who would hold the instrument for His death. While the Roman soldiers (and we) were yet sinners, Christ was dying for them (Rom. 5:8).

STUDY QUESTIONS:

◆ Paul declared that Jesus came into the world at "just the right moment." What about the moment in world history—where Romans ruled the world—made it an ideal time for Jesus to come to the earth?

◆ What unique claims did Jesus make about Himself that would separate Christianity from the pagan religions of the Romans?

◆ Compare and contrast the power of the Roman Empire and the humble power of Jesus.

◆ Consider Jesus' forgiveness of the Roman soldiers who executed Him and mocked Him below the cross.

◆ Meditate on the faith of the Roman centurion whose servant Jesus healed and the faith of the Roman centurion at the foot of the cross who declared Jesus to be the Son of God. What does this say about God's plan to draw people from every nation, tribe, and tongue?

SUGGESTED HYMNS AND SONGS:

Jesus Paid It All—Elvina Hall
Amazing Grace—John Newton

So we've walked through some of the characters of Easter, the otherwise ordinary characters who were swept up into the most important events in the history of the world, at "just the right moment" when God chose to send Jesus Christ into the world to save sinners.

As you contemplate the cross and the empty tomb this Easter, as you gather with your family and your friends, I encourage you to put yourself in the sandals of those who witnessed the miracle of the resurrection in the first century and think about how you might see yourself in their lives.

Perhaps you, like Peter, are compelled by Jesus but stumble along the way and have denied Him in your worst moments. Maybe you are limping into this holiday with a heavy heart, burdened by the weight of your sin. I encourage you to look at the cross where Jesus bore that sin, and look toward the empty tomb where Jesus rose victoriously so you could have new life.

You might be a bit like John, coming first to Jesus with bravado and scorn for anyone who doesn't see it your way. Perhaps you still see others the way this former Son of Thunder did. But it's not too late for the resurrection to envelop your heart and turn you into a disciple of love.

You might be approaching Easter like Thomas, longing for intimacy with the Almighty but harboring doubts about God's goodness, at times willing to die for Jesus and yet also plagued by questions. This year perhaps you will see a glimpse of Jesus' nail-scarred hands and declare Jesus to be "my Lord and my God!"

You could also be Judas—having been close to Jesus and known the language of faith, but finding yourself disillusioned because you have not experienced the Jesus you wanted. Unlike Judas, you don't have to let the last chapter of your life end in despair. You can look to the one who is willing to forgive your sins and betrayals and welcome you home again.

Maybe you are like Pilate; for your whole life you have tried to avoid the question of Jesus but He keeps pursuing you. You can choose to embrace the false notion that truth is unavailable, or you can yield to the mystery and pursue the one who is pursuing you.

Or you could be a secret disciple, like Joseph or Nicodemus. Today might be the day that, like them, you risk it all and declare your allegiance to the one who died and rose again for you.

Ultimately all of us are Barabbas, guilty of crimes for which we should be punished by a just and righteous God. And yet standing in our place, taking our punishment, bearing our sin is the Innocent One, Jesus.

This Jesus not only died for our sins. If we listen closely to the words of those first witnesses, the faithful women who saw the agony of the cross and the joy of the resurrection, we should not seek the living among the dead. Jesus is risen, and today He is as alive as He has ever been. And because Jesus is alive, everything has changed, reconciliation with God is possible, and God is renewing and restoring all things. There is a better world to come. I pray you experience that reality this Easter.

ACKNOWLEDGMENTS

I want to thank my agent, Erik Wolgemuth, and his entire team for continually partnering with me to do gospel work through my writing career. I want to thank my good friend Drew Dyck, who has opened so many doors for me. I want to thank Betsey Newenhuyse, who is an editor extraordinaire who helps make prose read like poetry. I'm also grateful for my church, Green Hill Church in Mt. Juliet, where we gather weekly to remind ourselves of the glorious truth that Christ has risen from the grave. I want to thank my wife and kids for allowing me to ignore them for long stretches while hunched over my laptop pounding out this book.

The essence of this book is the essence of our faith: Because Jesus of Nazareth has risen from the grave, so too will we rise one day, body and soul. Death has been defeated and God is, in Jesus, renewing and restoring the world. We can have peace with God. This Easter, let's rise up and celebrate.

N O T E S

Introduction: Why We Need Easter

1. Jaroslav Pelikan, "In Memoriam Faculty," Yale Department of History Newsletter (Spring 2007), 3.
2. Tish Harrison Warren, "If Easter Is Only a Symbol, Then to Hell with It," *Christianity Today*, April 9, 2020, https://www.christianitytoday.com/ct/2020/april-web-only/coronavirus-easter-only-symbol-then-hell-with-it.html.
3. N. T. Wright, *Surprised by Hope: Rethinking Heaven, the Resurrection, and the Mission of the Church* (New York: HarperOne, 2008), 293.
4. Warren, "If Easter Is Only a Symbol, Then to Hell with It."

Chapter One ✦ The Failure: Peter

1. Charles R. Swindoll, *Jesus: The Greatest Life of All* (Nashville: Thomas Nelson, 2009), 272.
2. Jason Isbell and the 400 Unit, "What've I Done to Help," *Reunions*, 2020.

Chapter Two ✦ The Beloved: John

1. As quoted in Doremus Almy Hayes, *John and His Writings* (New York: The Methodist Book Concern, 1917), 77.
2. D. A. Carson, *The Gospel according to John*, The Pillar New Testament Commentary (Leicester, England: Apollos, 1991), 146.
3. William L. Lane, *The Gospel according to Mark: The English Text with Introduction, Exposition, and Notes*, 2nd rev. ed. (Grand Rapids, MI: Eerdmans, 1974), 68.
4. N. T. Wright and Michael Bird, *The New Testament in Its World: An Introduction to the History, Literature, and Theology of the First Christians*, (London: Zondervan Academic, 2019), 113.
5. John MacArthur, *Matthew 1–7*, The MacArthur New Testament Commentary (Chicago: Moody Press, 1985), 117.
6. Warren W. Wiersbe, *Be Compassionate (Luke 1–13): Let the World Know That Jesus Cares* (Colorado Springs: David C. Cook, 2010), 128.

7. Charles Haddon Spurgeon, "The Disciple Whom Jesus Loved," May 23, 1880, http://www.spurgeon.org/resource-library/sermons/the-disciple-whom-jesus-loved.

8. Polycarp, quoted in J. C. Robertson, *Sketches of Church History: From A.D. 33 to the Reformation* (London: Society for Promoting Christian Knowledge, 1895), 14.

Chapter Three ✦ The Betrayer: Judas

1. Merrill C. Tenney, *John: The Gospel of Belief: An Analytic Study of the Text* (Grand Rapids, MI: Eerdmans, 1948), 202.

2. Colin Smith, "4 Things We Can Learn from Judas," The Gospel Coalition, March 29, 2018, https://www.thegospelcoalition.org/article/4-things-learn-judas/.

3. Charles R. Swindoll, ed., *The Living Insights Study Bible*, 1st ed. (Grand Rapids, MI: Zondervan, 1996), 1136.

4. Karl Barth, *Church Dogmatics: The Doctrine of God, Volume 2, Part 2: The Election of God; The Command of God* (Bloomsbury Publishing, 2003), 463.

5. Manlio Simonetti, ed., *Matthew 1–13*, Ancient Christian Commentary on Scripture (Downers Grove, IL: IVP Academic, 2001), 271.

6. Michael Green, *The Message of Matthew* (London: SPCK, 2014), 273.

7. Walter C. Kaiser Jr. and Duane Garrett, eds., *NIV Archaeological Study Bible: An Illustrated Walk Through Biblical History and Culture* (Grand Rapids, MI: Zondervan, 2006), 1618.

8. Michael Wilcock and John R. W Stott, ed., *The Message of Luke (The Bible Speaks Today Series)* (Downers Grove, IL: InterVarsity Press, 1979), 192.

9. John Calvin, *Calvin's Commentaries*, vol. 18, John 12–21, Acts 1–15, trans. William Pringle (Grand Rapids, MI: Baker Books, 2005), 190.

10. C. J. Allen, ed., *The Broadman Bible Commentary* (Nashville: Broadman, 1970), 330.

11. Smith, "4 Things We Can Learn from Judas."

12. Thomas R. Schreiner, *New Testament Theology: Magnifying God in Christ* (Grand Rapids, MI: Baker Academic, 2008), 271.

Chapter Four ✦ The Rogue: Barabbas

1. Joel C. Elowsky, ed., and Thomas C. Oden, gen. ed., *John 11–21 in Ancient Christian Commentary on Scripture: New Testament IVb* (Downers Grove, IL: InterVarsity Press, 2007), 211.

2. Darrell L. Bock, *Luke 9:51–24:53*, vol. 2, Baker Exegetical Commentary on the New Testament (Grand Rapids, MI: Baker Academic, 1996), 1831.

3. Sinclair B. Ferguson, *Let's Study Mark*, vol. 2, Let's Study Series (Carlisle, PA: Banner of Truth Trust, 1999), 257.

Chapter Five ✦ The Powerless: Pilate

1. N. T. Wright and Michael Bird, *The New Testament in Its World: An Introduction to the History, Literature, and Theology of the First Christians* (London: Zondervan Academic, 2019), 96–99.

2. Mark L. Strauss, *Four Portraits, One Jesus: An Introduction to Jesus and the Gospels* (Grand Rapids, MI: Zondervan, 2007), 496.

3. Walter C. Kaiser Jr. and Duane Garrett, eds., *NIV Archaeological Study Bible: An Illustrated Walk Through Biblical History and Culture* (Grand Rapids, MI: Zondervan, 2006), 1632.

4. Flavius Josephus, *Antiquities of the Jews*, 18.60, trans. William Whiston, accessed June 9, 2020, https://lexundria.com/j_aj/18.60/wst.

5. D. A. Carson, *The Gospel according to John*, The Pillar New Testament Commentary (Leicester, England: Apollos, 1991), 595.

6. Merrill C. Tenney, *John: The Gospel of Belief: An Analytic Study of the Text* (Grand Rapids, MI: Eerdmans, 1948),

7. Wright and Bird, *The New Testament in Its World*.

8. Alistair Begg, "Pilate Asks a Crucial Question: Who Is Jesus? (1 of 7)," YouTube, posted March 25, 2018, https://www.youtube.com/watch?v=b_ovyW3gEMI.

Chapter Six ✦ The Doubter: Thomas

1. Charles Haddon Spurgeon, "The Evidence of Our Lord's Wounds," December 2, 1877, The Spurgeon Center, https://www.spurgeon.org/resource-library/sermons/the-evidence-of-our-lords-wounds#flipbook/.

2. Russ Ramsey, *Behold the King of Glory: A Narrative of the Life, Death, and Resurrection of Jesus Christ* (Wheaton, IL: Crossway, 2015), 219.

3. Nicole Cliffe, "How God Messed Up My Happy Atheist Life," *Christianity Today*, May 20, 2016, https://www.christianitytoday.com/ct/2016/june/nicole-cliffe-how-god-messed-up-my-happy-atheist-life.html.

4. D. A. Carson, *The Gospel according to John*, The Pillar New Testament Commentary (Leicester, England: Apollos, 1991), 659.

5. Merrill C. Tenney, *John: The Gospel of Belief: An Analytic Study of the Text* (Grand Rapids, MI: Eerdmans, 1948), 284.

Chapter Seven ✦ The Religious: The Pharisees, Scribes, and Sadducees

1. N. T. Wright and Michael Bird, *The New Testament in Its World: An Introduction to the History, Literature, and Theology of the First Christians* (London: Zondervan Academic, 2019), 330–31.
2. Charlie Daniels Band, "New Pharisees," *Steel Witness*, 1996.
3. Walter C. Kaiser Jr. and Duane Garrett, eds., *NIV Archaeological Study Bible: An Illustrated Walk Through Biblical History and Culture* (Grand Rapids, MI: Zondervan, 2006), 1704.
4. Wright and Bird, *The New Testament in Its World*, 125.
5. Thomas R. Schreiner, *New Testament Theology: Magnifying God in Christ* (Grand Rapids, MI: Baker Academic, 2008), 515.
6. Timothy Keller, *The Prodigal God: Recovering the Heart of the Christian Faith*, reprint ed. (New York: Penguin Books, 2011), 75.

Chapter Eight ✦ The Witnesses: The Women at the Tomb

1. Arthur A. Just Jr., ed., and Thomas C. Oden, gen. ed., *Luke in Ancient Christian Commentary: New Testament III* (Downers Grove, IL: InterVarsity Press, 2003), 374.
2. Leon Morris, *The Gospel according to Matthew* (Grand Rapids, MI: Eerdmans, 1992), 726.
3. Leon Morris, ed., *Luke: An Introduction and Commentary* (Grand Rapids, MI: Eerdmans, 1988), 169.
4. Chad Brand, Eric Mitchel, and Holman Reference Editorial Staff, eds., *Holman Illustrated Bible Dictionary*, revised and expanded (Nashville: B&H Publishing Group, 2015).
5. Bruce Chilton and Jacob Neusner, *The Brother of Jesus: James the Just and His Mission* (Philadelphia: Westminster John Knox Press, 2001), 20.
6. N. T. Wright and Michael Bird, *The New Testament in Its World: An Introduction to the History, Literature, and Theology of the First Christians* (London: Zondervan Academic, 2019), 318–19.
7. R. T. France, *The Gospel of Matthew* in *The New International Commentary on the New Testament* (Grand Rapids, MI: Eerdmans, 2007).
8. Richard Bauckham, *Jesus and the Eyewitnesses: The Gospels as Eyewitness Testimony*, 2nd ed. (Grand Rapids, MI: Eerdmans, 2017), 49.

9. Andreas J. Köstenberger and Justin Taylor, "Five Errors to Drop From Your Easter Sermon," *Christianity Today*, April 15, 2014, https://www.christianitytoday.com/ct/2014/april-web-only/five-errors-to-drop-from-your-easter-sermon.html.

10. Wright and Bird, *The New Testament in Its World*, 319.

Chapter Nine ✦ The Secret Disciples: Nicodemus and Joseph of Arimathea

1. Paul Tripp, "The Lesser Known Joseph," PaulTripp.com, March 26, 2018, https://www.paultripp.com/articles/posts/the-lesser-known-joseph.

2. "Brother Andrew's Story," Open Doors USA, accessed June 27, 2020, https://www.opendoorsusa.org/about-us/history/brother-andrews-story/.

3. "Nicodemus Comes to Jesus," Ligonier Ministries, accessed June 27, 2020, https://www.ligonier.org/learn/devotionals/nicodemus-comes-to-jesus/?.

4. Walter C. Kaiser Jr. and Duane Garrett, eds., *NIV Archaeological Study Bible: An Illustrated Walk Through Biblical History and Culture* (Grand Rapids, MI: Zondervan, 2006), 1616.

5. Ibid., 1660.

6. Merrill C. Tenney, *John: The Gospel of Belief: An Analytic Study of the Text* (Grand Rapids, MI: Eerdmans, 1948),

Chapter Ten ✦ The Executioners: Who Were the Romans?

1. R. Kent Hughes, *Luke (2 Volumes in 1 / ESV Edition): That You May Know the Truth* (Wheaton, IL: Crossway, 2014), 814.

2. Andreas J. Köstenberger, Leonard Scott Kellum, and Charles L. Quarles, *The Cradle, the Cross, and the Crown: An Introduction to the New Testament* (Nashville: B&H Publishing Group, 2009), 79.

3. N. T. Wright and Michael Bird, *The New Testament in Its World: An Introduction to the History, Literature, and Theology of the First Christians* (London: Zondervan Academic, 2019), 153.

4. Ibid., 155.

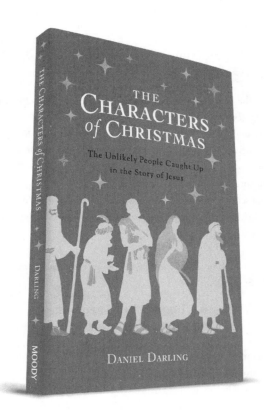

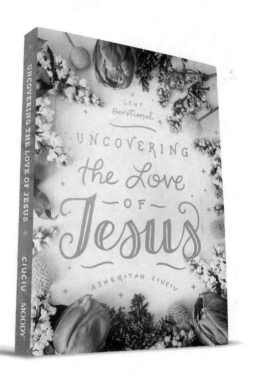

MOODY
Publishers®

From the Word to Life®

Reclaim the Lenten season with 40 devotionals that reveal the deep love of Jesus poured out for us. Each daily reflection looks at Jesus' personal interactions in Scripture and leads you in meditation on a new aspect of His love. Don't let Easter pass you by this year.

978-0-8024-1949-1 | also available as eBook and audiobook

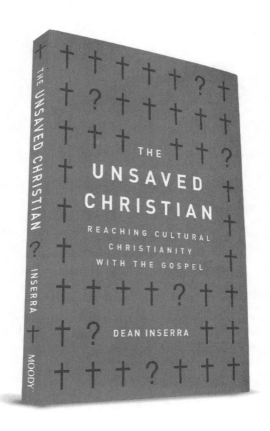